#4226 at Bellows Falls, Vermont. May 2, 1965. *(Russell Munroe)*

Boston and Maine *In Color*

by
Jeremy F. Plant and Jeffrey G. Plant

Published by
Morning Sun Books, Inc.
9 Pheasant Lane
Scotch Plains, NJ 07076

Library of Congress
Catalog Card No. 96-078482

First Printing
ISBN 1-878887-74-2

Color separation and printing by
The Kutztown Publishing Co., Inc.
Kutztown, Pennsylvania

Acknowledgements

The Boston & Maine: what was a railroad with this name doing in New York State? As children in Troy, New York, the B&M seemed out of place, not a natural part of New York like the New York Central or the Delaware & Hudson, our other local railroads. Saturday mornings at Troy Union Station or near our aunt's house in North Troy in the midcentury years established a lasting love affair with this interloper from New England. The Troy Branch that brought B&M trains into town was then a fairly busy line, and a typical day would feature a freight with FT's, perhaps a Rutland milk train, and passenger trains with E-7s or our favorite B&M equipment, Unit #6000, the ZEPHYR-like MINUTE MAN. Occasional rides up the Hoosic Valley or over into western Massachusetts on the Mohawk Trail became opportunities to see the B&M in action.

Things changed rapidly and totally in Troy in the late 1950's with the closing of Troy Union Station. It was not until we became mobile on our own in the 1960's that we discovered nearby Mechanicville Yard and the thrill of chasing trains through the Hoosic Valley. For Jeff, college in the early 1960's in Medford afforded a chance to see the B&M in its home territory.

The mid-1970's found us both living and working in the Albany area. The B&M was entering a productive and interesting era under the inspired leadership of Alan Dustin. Along with its neighbor and partner, the Delaware & Hudson, the B&M of the 1970's and early 1980's provided pleasant surprise after pleasant surprise: unit coal trains, bicentennial paint schemes, runthrough power, and always plenty of trains.

What follows is a photographic portrayal of the B&M in the era of color photography. The organization is by time period, reflecting the changes in the operations, equipment, architecture, and the economy of the regions served by the Boston & Maine. What emerges is the gradual transformation of the road from a maze of lines serving almost all parts of Northern New England to an X of two major routes, an east-west route from Portland and Boston to the western connections in New York State, and a north-south route linking central Massachusetts with Canada and uppermost Vermont and New Hampshire.

Our sincerest appreciation and thanks go to Bob Yanosey of Morning Sun, for fostering and facilitating this venture, and to the photographers whose book it truly is: Jack Armstrong, Charles Ballard, John Bartley, George Berisso, Steve Bogan, William Brennan, James Buckley, Gardiner Cross, Matthew Herson, Al Holtz, Ed Kelsey, T. J. McNamara, Bill Mischler, Russell Munroe, Jr., James Odell, Brian Plant, Jonathan Plant, Tom Post, Donald Robinson, Jim Shaughnessy, J. W. Swanberg, Frank Watson, Bob Wilt, Jack Wright, Walter Zullig; the Don Ball Collection, Bob's Photo, the Bill Volkmer Collection, the Bob Wilt Collection, the Bob Yanosey Collection. Special thanks to Martin Butler for his help in locating photographs; to the Boston & Maine Historical Society for their excellent publications and reference material; to the published writers on the Boston & Maine, including Harry Frye, Scott Hartley, Robert Willoughby Jones, Tom Nelligan, and David Sweetland; and to our family for encouraging us.

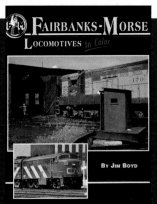

Boston and Maine *In Color*

Northern New England: a region of great diversity compressed into a geographic area not much bigger than a medium-sized state in other parts of the country. Four states: Maine, New Hampshire, Vermont, and Massachusetts. It's possible to divide New England into two different parts, a Southern New England of sandy shores, large cities, and a generally flat coastal plain topography, and a wilder and less populated Northern New England of mountains, rushing streams, rocky coasts, and small self-sufficient villages: the New England of Robert Frost. Centering and cementing the equation is the great city of Boston, the metropolis of New England, and the state of Massachusetts, possessing qualities of each of the two subregions.

The railroad picture reinforced the differences between Southern and Northern New England. The Boston & Albany line of the New York Central cut straight through the dividing line of North and South, and was anyway seen as a little suspect by New Englanders jealous of their region's autonomy. Conceived by Bostonians eager to connect their city with the riches of the West it fell under the control of the New York Central and so assumed its modern image as an interloper, controlled by New York, not New Englanders. More fitting the image of the two New Englands was the convenient

way that the region's two indigenous trunk lines, the New Haven and the Boston & Maine, controlled their hemispheres of the known world, the New Haven, with the exception of its line to Lowell keeping south of the line formed by the east-west mainline of the B&M, the latter road controlling the major north-south routes to Portland and up the Connecticut River, and west along the hills of Northern Massachusetts to the upper Hudson and Mohawk Valleys of New York. Smaller roads like the Maine Central and Bangor and Aroostook, and the Canadian-controlled roads like Central Vermont, Grand Trunk, and the CP's own routes in Vermont and Maine, were relevant but lacked the omnipresent character of the New Haven and B&M in their respective halves of the New England whole.

In the 1940's and early 1950's, the operations of the B&M reflected the need to carry out four distinct and important roles for its Northern New England region. The first was to funnel passengers to and from the great metropolis of Boston, both to immediate suburban communities for day-workers and to more distant communities that looked to Boston as a place to visit, to shop, to do business. Second, the B&M served the greater Boston area and industrialized Merrimack Valley as a terminal

(Below) #3648 laying over for weekend at Reading, MA. 3/20/55 *(Russell Munroe)*

freight road, servicing local industries and docks and interchanging with connecting roads. Third, it linked the small towns of its lines, especially branchlines, with the outside world, for freight, mail, milk, and passenger service. Fourth, and final, it provided a bridge for freight (and some long-distance passengers) to other regions. The major connections were in all four compass directions: east at Portland with the Maine Central, and through it to the Bangor and Aroostook; south, at Boston, Worcester, and Springfield with the New Haven; north, at Bellows Falls with the Rutland and on the Connecticut River line with the Central Vermont and Canadian Pacific; and west, at Mechanicville and Rotterdam Junction with the Delaware & Hudson and New York Central.

Operations were divided into four divisions. The Terminal Division handled the extensive terminal operations of the greater Boston area. The Portland Division consisted of both the Western and Eastern Routes up the coast to Maine. The New Hampshire Division consisted of the New Hampshire Mainline north of North Billerica, the White Mountains Line, and various branches in the Granite State. The Fitchburg Division consisted of the Fitchburg Mainline, the Connecticut River Line, the Troy Branch, the Cheshire Branch, and a few other branches. Major yards were Rigby in South Portland, operated in conjunction with Maine Central and joint affiliate Portland Terminal; East Deerfield, at the junction of the Conn River and Fitchburg Mainline; Mechanicville, the major interchange point with the Delaware & Hudson and major West End shop facility. Smaller yards were scattered all over the system, at Lawrence, Springfield, Concord, Woodsville, White River Junction, Troy, Berlin, Salem, Portsmouth, Worcester, and other points.

The history of the Boston & Maine Railroad begins in 1835, with a charter to build part of a railroad from Boston to Portland, ME. After completion of the line from Boston to the Maine/New Hampshire border at South Berwick, ME the B&M began to acquire most of the independent railroads in Northern Massachusetts, Southern Maine, and New Hampshire: the Eastern Railroad, its competitor for the Boston to Maine traffic, in 1884; the Boston & Lowell in 1887, giving the B&M virtual domination of traffic to New Hampshire; the Concord & Montreal and Connecticut River Railroads in the early 1890's, giving B&M a strong position in the Upper Connecticut Valley and White Mountains; and, in 1900, the Fitchburg Railroad, giving the B&M its final new mainline across the northern part of Massachusetts to western connections at Troy, Mechanicville, and Rotterdam Junction, NY. A number of branches were acquired along with the mainlines, making the B&M a spiderweb of trackage in Northern New England.

The modern history of the Boston & Maine begins with the progressive administration of George Hannauer. Mr. Hannauer assumed the presidency of the road in 1927, coming from the presidency of the Indiana Harbor Belt. He immediately began a modernization program for the railroad, including the installation of Centralized Traffic Control on major sections of the mainlines; construction of modern hump yards at East Deerfield,

Mechanicville, and Boston; purchase of 25 "superpower" 2-8-4 freight engines to supplant the 2-8-0's and lumbering 2-10-2's in mainline freight service; and perhaps most dramatically, the building of the modern North Station and affiliated hotel and athletic facilities on Causeway Street in Boston. Hannauer was succeeded in 1931 by Edward S. French, a Vermonter with an extensive career in New England railroading. E. S. or "Ned" French continued the progressive spirit on the B&M but according to most sources, with a more humane management philosophy than his predecessor. The French era on the B&M spanned twenty years, 1931 - 1951: some would say the finest twenty years in the B&M's history.

Under French the B&M acquired control of the Maine Central, its major feeder line; trimmed unproductive branch lines; acquired more modern steam engines, the well-proportioned P-4 Pacifics and R-1 Mountains; introduced New England to the age of streamliners with the FLYING YANKEE; dieselized early and effectively its major freight and passenger operations, concentrating steam on branch lines and Boston commuter runs; and promoted Northern New England as a vacation destination. The B&M in the French era was a New England friend and neighbor, promising reliability, clean and comfortable trains, and frequent service. A balancing of the old with the new, traditions and innovations.

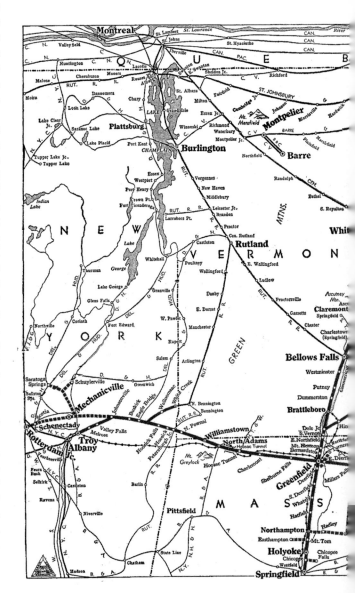

By the 1950's, it was clear that New England railroads were in for major and troubling changes. The automobile and the truck were cutting deeply into the demand for passenger and freight service on the road's network of lines. Major road construction, halted during the war years, caught up with demand in the 1950's as the Massachusetts Turnpike, Maine Turnpike, and interstate highways paralleled the B&M's routes. The B&M, it has been said, "went from somewhere to nowhere": from the populous Boston region to connections with other roads at out of the way places like Mechanicville, Wells River, White River Junction, Troy. Only the Boston-Portland route went "somewhere to somewhere," connecting the biggest cities of Maine and Massachusetts and providing the only direct rail link between Maine and the rest of the country.

The regime of Patrick McGinnis, starting in 1956, accelerated the downward trend of the road. McGinnis was a securities broker, a finance man oriented toward bottom lines. After a successful stint at the Norfolk Southern (the drowsy shortline, not the current major NS), McGinnis embarked on a bold plan to build a New England rail empire, beginning with the New Haven in 1954. It was not to be. More than any other part of the country, New England was seeing the decline of railroading, with high fixed costs of terminal and commuter operations, short mainline hauls, a declining manufacturing base, and a virtual collapse of short and medium distance passenger service.

If the French era was a juggling of the old and new, the McGinnis years were a brutal renunciation of the traditions that had formed the image (and self-image) of the Boston & Maine. In 1956, the last steam operations ended, and the B&M continued the process of replacing all locomotive-hauled trains with Budd "Highliners." Passenger service died rapidly: to Troy and the Cheshire in 1958, to Bangor in 1960, even Portland by 1964. The traditional maroon and gold "Minute Man" livery was replaced by a blue-black-white scheme and a new BM logo. North Station became a shadow of its former self, with tracks replaced for parking lots. Maintenance was reduced, more branch lines eliminated, service reduced. The operating ratio improved, but the old B&M, the blanket drawn around the Northern New England region, was gone.

McGinnis was gone by 1962, after five years of operating losses and a growing disenchantment among the B&M's stockholders with his approach to the road. He would be brought to trial for fraudulent business practices and serve a year and a half behind bars. By the 1960's the B&M was hanging on, a shadow of its former self. Traffic remained steady on the main routes, but the

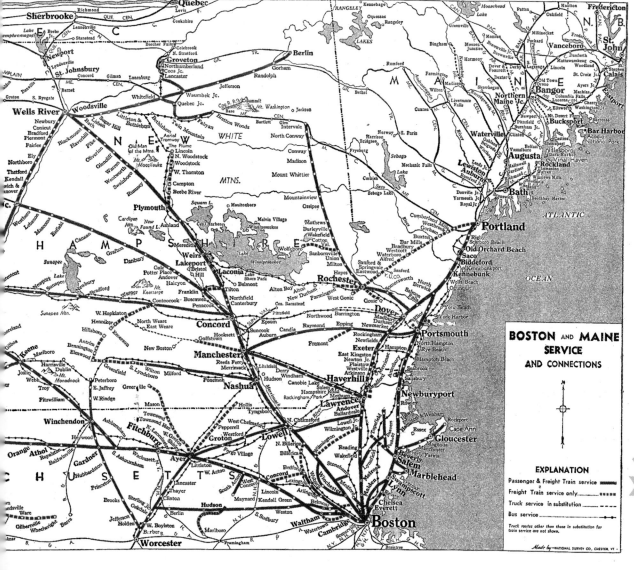

(Above) #4256 at Somerville Yard, Boston, MA July 1963

costs of operating a short-haul bridge and terminal rail-road were mounting. The mileage continued to be trimmed as branches and even some former mainlines were no longer profitable. The Fitchburg Division was the life-saver, as Maine replaced Boston as the major destination of bridge traffic. The GP-9's that McGinnis acquired in 1957 to replace the aging FT's seemed anti-quated as mainline power in the second generation of diesel development. Track conditions deteriorated, and the B&M seemed to be on the well-worn road to oblivion. Merger or bankruptcy seemed the alternatives faced by the road.

In early 1970 the hammer fell. The B&M was unable to meet payment on first mortgage bonds; its operating deficit was climbing, reaching $5.5 million in the six months prior; it had $115 million in debt and only $15 million in assets. Creditors demanded liquidation. Like most Eastern roads, the B&M had seemingly run out of options to crawl out of the downward spiral of debt and decline.

Enter some extraordinary individuals and fortuitous developments. Court-appointed trustees Robert W. Meserve and Charles W. Bartlett, working with able new management, came up with a plan approved by the ICC to keep the B&M going for enough time to get it back on its feet. A series of effective presidents, beginning with the legendary John W. Barriger in 1971 and continuing with Paul

Cherington in 1973, got the operating deficits down and the confidence of shippers back. The Massachusetts Bay Transportation Authority came up with a generous plan to remove the burden of commuter operations from the road. After the ICC rejected both a merger with Norfolk & Western (which did not want the debt-ridden B&M) and liquidation, the next challenge was the government's plan to consolidate the bankrupt Eastern carriers into a large, subsidized new system. The trustees in 1973 convinced the bankruptcy court that inclusion of the B&M in the Conrail merger would not be in the best interests of the road, averting what surely would have been wholesale abandonment of sections of the railroad.

Under Alan Dustin, who assumed the presidency in 1974, the B&M continued its remarkable recovery. Thirteen new GP38-2's, the first new units since 1961, helped both the image and the movement of freight between Mechanicville and Portland. The deal with MBTA was consummated to the satisfaction of all parties, and on 1/1/77 the B&M became the operator for the Boston commuter operation, but free of the onerous burden of ownership and operating losses. New GP40-2's put into service at the beginning of 1978 speeded up schedules and continued the modernization of the creaky B&M diesel fleet.

The responsibility of the trustees and management to put the B&M's house in order by 1978 had been met. The B&M now offered the potential for profit for new

investors. One of these, Timothy Mellon, purchased all of B&M's common stock for $24,250,000 which, added to the road's cash reserve and the MBTA purchase, brought an ending to the road's bankruptcy problems few would have dreamed of in the dark days of 1970. However, it also put an end to the remarkable recovery under Alan Dustin and the upbeat mood of the late 1970's.

This, then, was the Boston & Maine: a road of contrasts. Old and new; city and country; mainline and branchline; maroon and gold, and blue and black. Our trip begins before World War II and ends with today's Guilford and MBTA.

(Below) #1750 at Charlemont, MA July 1966.
(William J. Brennan)

Boston and Maine *In Color* Table of Contents

BOSTON and MAINE RAILROAD

(All three photos) Boston, March 1953.
(Don Ball collection)

B&M
Steam Roster

Type	Class	Number Series	Dates Built	Builder
0-6-0	G-10	200-309	1903-10	Manchester
	G-11	400-429	1911-13	Manchester
	G-11-b	430-452	1916	Brooks
	G-11-c	830-832, 834	1917-20	Schenectady
0-8-0	H-2-a	610-631	1922	Schenectady
	H-3-a	640-649	1927	Baldwin
	H-3-b	650-654	1929	Baldwin
2-6-0	B-15	1360-1431, 1435-1459	1903-07	Manchester
	B-15-a	1460-1499	1909-10	Schenectady, Manchester
2-8-0	K-7-a	2390-2429	1907-11	Schenectady
	K-8-a	2600-2639	1911	Baldwin
	K-8-b	2640-2709	1913	Baldwin/Schen.
	K-8-c	2710-2734	1916	Brooks
4-4-2	J-1-b	3220-3244	1908-09	Manchester
4-6-2	P-2-a	3620-3659	1911	Schenectady
	P-2-b	3660-3679	1913	Schenectady
	P-2-c	3680-3689	1916	Schenectady
	P-5-a	3696-3699	1924	Brooks
	P-3-a	3700-3709	1923	Schenectady
	P-4-a	3710-3714	1934	Lima
	P-4-b	3715-3719	1937	Lima
4-8-2	R-1-a	4100-4104	1935	Baldwin
	R-1-b	4105-4109	1937	Baldwin
	R-1-c	4110-4112	1939	Baldwin
	R-1-d	4113-4117	1941	Baldwin
2-8-4	T-1-a	4000-4019	1928	Lima
	T-1-b	4020-4024	1929	Lima

(Above) Boston, July 1956. (Al Holtz)
(Below) Mechanicville. (Jim Shaughnessy)

B&M Diesel Roster

Type	Builder	Date	Road Numbers
AA	EMC	1935	6000
HH-660	Alco	1934-39	1160-1162
SC	EMC	1936	1103-1105
SW	EMC	1938	1106-1108
SW-1	EMD	1939-53	1109-1132
44ton	GE	1940-48	110-119
NW-2	EMD	1941-49	1200-1213
FT	EMD	1943-44	4200-4223 A/B
S-1	Alco	1944-49	1163-1172
S-2	Alco	1944-45	1260-1265
F-2	EMD	1946	4226 A/B; 4250-4264
E-7	EMD	1946-49	3800-3820
F-3	EMD	1948	4227-4228 A/B
BL-2	EMD	1948	1550-1553
RS-2	Alco	1948-49	1500-1504; 1530-1534
F-7	EMD	1949-50	4265-4268 A/B
S-3	Alco	1950-52	1173-1188
S-4	Alco	1950	1266-1281
GP-7	EMD	1950-53	1555-1577
SW-9	EMD	1952-53	1220-1231
RS-3	Alco	1952-55	1505-1519; 1535-1545
SW-8	EMD	1953	800-807
S-5	Alco	1954	860-865
GP-9	EMD	1957	1700-1749
P12-42	F-M	1957	1-2
GP-18	EMD	1961	1750-1755
GP-38-2	EMD	1973	201-212 (212 renumbered to 200)
GP-40-2	EMD	1977	300-317

(Above) Boston is a great circus town, and Boston Garden's proximity to North Station made the B&M a logical road to pull in the circus trains. One of the B&M's big T-1 2-8-4's is on the point of a Boston-bound circus train at Hastings, MA in the spring of 1939. The "Lima's," as the engines were called on the B&M, were put out of business on the Mechanicville runs by the FT's. Seventeen of the 25 were sold to the Santa Fe and the Southern Pacific in the last days of World War II, making color photographs of the T's rather unusual. *(Donald S. Robinson)*

The 1930's was a decade of troubles for American railroads, which were hit hard by the economic woes of the Great Depression. The B&M under the leadership of Edward French had weathered the difficult years quite well. In the words of David Morgan, the B&M "rolled up its sleeves and went to work with all the Yankee ingenuity and tenacity it could muster up." This included trimming trackage, capturing the public's fancy with the FLYING YANKEE streamliner and the naming of the new P-4 and R-1 steam engines, and acquiring control of one of its major feeder roads, the Maine Central. Morale among the road's employees was high and the future looked bright.

(Above) Before the arrival of the FT's during the war, the top freight assignments went to the 2-8-4's and 4-8-2's. In 1938 representatives of the two classes share the space at the East Deerfield engine facility with one of the K-8 2-8-0's used in pusher service on the Fitchburg Division. East Deerfield is at the junction of the Connecticut River Line and the east-west Fitchburg Division mainline, and so occupies one of the most critical locations on the Boston & Maine. *(Bob's Photos)*

The 1930's

(Left) A gas-electric unit is the consist for Train #3107 bound for Clinton on the Central Massachusetts Branch at Waverly on a snowy afternoon in 1939.
(Donald S. Robinson)

(Below) Unit #6000's 142-passenger capacity was not sufficient to handle the wartime demands of the Bangor-Boston run, and was reassigned in 1944 to the White River Junction-Boston CHESHIRE via Bellows Falls and the Cheshire Branch. It is seen here at Waverly in 1945, the serviceman at the right a reminder of the millions of men and women who served the nation during World War II. The CHESHIRE used the Fitchburg mainline from Boston to South Ashburnham, where it switched to the Cheshire Branch for the run through Winchendon and Keene to the Connecticut River. *(Donald S. Robinson)*

Self-Propelled Trains

World War II brought new levels of freight traffic to the Boston & Maine, along with most other American railroads. B&M was a critical link in the flow of eastbound war materiel to east coast destinations, including oil, food, war machinery, and vehicles. To sustain the flow of traffic, especially on the Mechanicville mainline, the B&M successfully convinced the War Production Board that it needed to put into operation the coveted FT cab freight units manufactured by EMD. Six 2,700 A/B sets arrived in 1943 and 18 more in 1944 to dominate the manifests between Mechanicville, Portland, Boston, and Worcester. Adorned in the maroon-and-gold colors that it initiated on the road, the bulldog-nosed freight cabs, operating in two or four unit sets won the war for the B&M. They had the advantage over the steamers of being able to operate through the 4.75 miles of Hoosac Tunnel without the need to add the electric units, speeding up the movement of freight and eventually rendering that expensive service unnecessary. The success of the FT's made the B&M look to EMD for all its freight and passenger cab units purchased between 1945 and 1950, even though American Locomotive Company in Schenectady was almost adjacent to the Western Gateway Line to Rotterdam.

(Above) The war is over and the FT's are beginning to invade the Connecticut River Line in this 1946 shot by Donald Robinson of White River Junction - Springfield freight JS-2 at Greenfield. The units wear the original FT color scheme, a unique lettering shield on each flank and no Minute Man on the nose. B&M was the only New England railroad to operate the four-portholed pioneer F units. *(Donald S. Robinson)*

(Above) The phenomenal success of the FT's convinced B&M management that EMD road diesels were the hope of the future. Cessation of hostilities in 1945 allowed the domestic diesel locomotive industry to resume normal production of passenger units. The B&M ordered a total of 22 E units between 1945 and 1950; the first 21 were the 2,000 horsepower E-7 model, the last, #3821, the only example of the 2,250 horsepower E-8. Delivered in four batches beginning in 1945, the E-7's were assigned to the long distances runs to Portland, Troy, and White River Junction. The large order of E-7's delivered in 1946 wore the short-lived "East Wind" or "Rock Island" scheme reminiscent of, but somewhat less gaudy than the contemporary "Rocket" scheme of the midwestern road. Two brand-new E-7's are at the Greenfield station with Train #54 from Troy in 1946. The Greenfield station was at the junction of the East-West Mainline and the Connecticut River Line and served both lines until the end of passenger service. *(Donald S. Robinson)*

(Below) The 3801 is also on Troy to Boston Train #54 making the stop at Greenfield, where passengers can make connections for Connecticut Valley locations. The 3801 illustrates the Minute Man scheme that was eventually applied to all the E units, in the opinion of most a better match for the lines of the handsome EMD cab units and the B&M's maroon passenger equipment. Delivery of the E-7's allowed dieselization of all operations on the West End between East Deerfield and Mechanicville, causing the cessation of the Hoosac Tunnel electric operation on August 23, 1946. The B&M became one of the first railroads to dieselize an entire operating district. *(Donald S. Robinson)*

(Above) P-4-b Pacific #3715, a 1937 product of Lima Locomotive Works, awaits the highball at North Station sometime after the end of World War II. The P-4's were extraordinarily handsome engines, their sleek lines enhanced by the shaded lettering and striping on the running boards and tender. Note the nameplate attached to the running board, and the engine's name, *Kwasind*. In 1937 the B&M sponsored a student contest to name the P-4 Pacifics and R-1 Mountains. The winners were announced as part of a ceremony at North Station on December 11, 1937. *Kwasind* was submitted by Charles Morrison, Jr., a student at the Center School in Danbury, NH. Each engine had a nameplate on each side of the engine, noting the name of the individual submitting the name and the name itself. *(Frank Watson)*

(Below) In dramatic contrast to the flashy road units was little 0-6-0 switcher #216, a G-10 class built by Manchester in 1904. *(Frank Watson)*

(Right) North Station in the 1940's was the place to find the new and the old in B&M passenger locomotion. The late afternoon light catches the maroon and gold paint of immaculate E-7 #3800, the B&M's first passenger diesel. Delivered in 1945, she was the first of 21 E-7's that, along with a single E-8 and a number of passenger-equipped F-2's, F-3's, and F-7's dominated the B&M's long-distance passenger runs in the postwar years. The sun angle and heavy head-end consist suggest that this may be Boston-Troy Train #59, the MINUTE MAN, but the photographer left no indication of what #3800's train was that faroff day. *(Frank Watson)*

(Below) Mogul #1427 heads out that same cloudless afternoon on an outbound commuter run. Was there ever a class of engine so emblematic of its owner as the B-15 2-6-0 on the Boston & Maine? One of 120 of the type built by Alco at its Manchester Works between 1903 and 1910, the 1427 and its kin are equally at home on Boston-area commuter runs and jack-of-all-trades assignments on the network of branchlines in north-central Massachusetts and southern New Hampshire called by observers "Mogul Country."

(Frank Watson)

North Station is close by the south bank of the Charles River. All trains entering and leaving the terminal passed over four lift bridges that provided entry to the 23-track stub-end station. This allowed simultaneous departure and arrival of trains destined for the various points on the system. The coincidence of commuter schedules with long-distance passenger arrival and departure times made the bridges the choke point for the busy station.

(Above) Frank Watson positioned himself on the east side of the tracks to make these well-lit pictures of morning trains entering North Station over the Charles River bridges. The 3624 is one of B&M's handsome P-2-a Pacifics, the workhorses of the B&M's steam passenger fleet.
(Frank Watson)

(Below) Two of the P-2 Pacifics are arriving simultaneously with morning inbound trains. Tower A, which controlled movements over the bridges, is the brick building visible in the background to the right of the bridges. *(Frank Watson)*

Charles River Bridges

(Above) It was unusual to see engines of the 2-8-0 wheel arrangement in commuter service, but it was not uncommon practice on the B&M. Consolidation #2403, class K-7-a, has another inbound commuter run in tow entering the station area, probably off the Stoneham Branch where this engine was assigned. *(Frank Watson)*

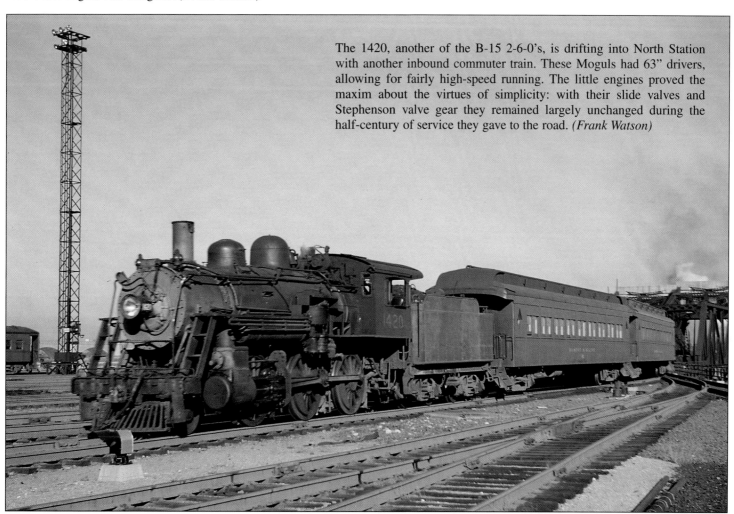

The 1420, another of the B-15 2-6-0's, is drifting into North Station with another inbound commuter train. These Moguls had 63" drivers, allowing for fairly high-speed running. The little engines proved the maxim about the virtues of simplicity: with their slide valves and Stephenson valve gear they remained largely unchanged during the half-century of service they gave to the road. *(Frank Watson)*

Maine and New Hampshire Passenger Service

(Left) Of all its passenger operations, the B&M invested most heavily after World War II in the service to Maine. Besides assigning the new E-7's to most of the runs, the road acquired 24 new coaches, combines, restaurant-parlor cars for the service to Portland and connections there with partner Maine Central for through service to Bangor, the Maritimes, and the Maine coast. The Western Route mainline on the 115 mile run from North Station to Portland was the closest thing the B&M had to a high-speed corridor, as shown here with a southbound train in the vicinity of Kingston, NH behind the 3806 in the summer of 1950. (Russell Munroe)

Presenting Our New Babies
Twelve Sets of Twins

AIR-CONDITIONING—Naturally these new super-deluxe coaches are air-conditioned. Many new features and improvements are included in the air-cleaning and circulating equipment. Ideally warm and cozy in Winter, Spring and Fall. Comfortably cool in Summer with all temperature controls automatic.

LIST OF NAMES—You'll find the individual names of all the 24 new cars listed in this leaflet. The youngsters who named them are proud of these names and we are proud that 240,000 youngsters in Maine, New Hampshire, Vermont and Massachusetts entered the naming contest.

WE INVITE COMMENT—The seats are the famous "Sleepy Hollow" chairs, designed after Professor Hooten of Harvard University measured over 1,000 travelers in the North Station to secure the best specifications to make a coach seat ideally comfortable for the average traveler. If you have suggestions for improvements in our service we'll be glad to receive constructive criticism.

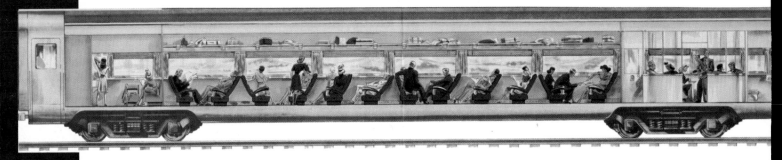

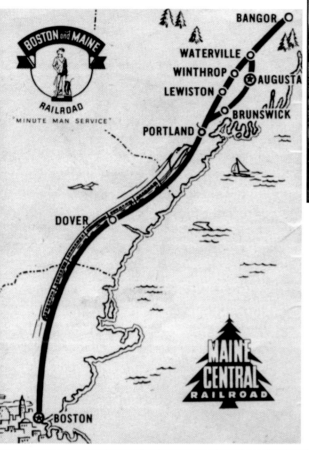

(Above) A less glamorous passenger service was operated on the Portsmouth Branch between Concord, Manchester and New Hampshire's port city at the mouth of the Piscataqua. Gas-electric units were common on the run, as seen here with unit #181 at Portsmouth on July 24, 1951. In later years, the run was cut back to Manchester and converted to a mixed train. *(James Buckley)*

(Left and below) The B&M was still confident about the future of passenger service Downeast in the late 1940's, as this upbeat promotional piece on the new passenger equipment suggests. Only someone with a crystal ball could guess that within a decade the B&M would be selling its passenger diesels and cars for scrap, and that a B&M president would end up in jail for the manner in which the deal was made. *(R.J. Yanosey collection)*

LOVELINESS—Even a man would use this feminine adjective in describing the appointments of these new cars. Soft colors in seats, walls, floors and ceilings blend in a pleasing combination that is easy on the eyes and restful in its simplicity.

INDIVIDUAL NAMES—Each of the new cars bears an individual name and the name of the Northern New England grammar school pupil who suggested it. The names will help you identify the car in which you are riding, if you leave the car at junction points for any reason.

NOT ENOUGH TO GO AROUND—While these new cars will provide super-deluxe accommodations on the Flying Yankee, the Pine Tree, and the Kennebec for normal patronage there may be times when some of our other air-conditioned coaches will have to be added. Use of the super-deluxe coaches will be on a first-come-first-served order.

(Right) Ayer was an important junction on the B&M, with several lines radiating out from the Fitchburg, including the Greenville and Hollis Branches to their namesake towns in southern New Hampshire. Most important was the Lowell-Worcester Line that provided a routing for traffic between Maine and southern New England through the New Haven connection at Worcester. E-7 #3804 is eastbound at Ayer with a train of New Haven coaches picked up at Worcester, perhaps a camp special bringing youngsters from New York to summer camp in the Pine Tree state.

(Russell Munroe)

(Below) Russell Munroe was beginning his distinguished photographic coverage of the Boston & Maine in 1950. A trip to Ayer, 36 miles west of Boston on the Fitchburg Line, yielded this magnificent portrait of K-8-c 2-8-0 #2719 on the point of a local freight. In 1949 the road reported that 86% of the freight traffic was handled by diesels, so we're fortunate to see part of the remainder still behind steam.

(Russell Munroe)

The Fitchburg Line in 1950

BOSTON and MAINE RAILROAD

(Above) The purchase of 18 F-2 A units and three B units in 1946 permitted the B&M to create A-B-A sets of 1,350 horsepower units. This three-unit configuration fit the horsepower needs of many of the B&M's freights, and offered savings in not having to turn or wye the sets that heretofore had been possible only in four-unit A-B-B-A sets. The 4207 A/B set leads F-2 #4258 westbound through Ayer bound for Mechanicville. *(Don Ball Collection)*

(Below) Most people associate mountains in Massachusetts with the Berkshire region in the far western part of the state. The Hoosac Tunnel eliminated most of the climb over the Berkshires, but the hilly stretch of north-central Massachusetts between Fitchburg and Gardner and East Deerfield required helpers, such as K-8-c 2-8-0 #2720, a 1919 purchase, pushing hard on a westbound. *(Don Ball Collection)*

(Above) Before the decline of passenger service on the B&M six trains each way were available to the traveler along the Connecticut Valley between Springfield and White River Junction. Train #74, the CONNECTICUT YANKEE, has made its 2:25 PM stop at Windsor, VT, the first scheduled stop below White River, behind 4-6-2 #3698. If the 3698 looks un-B&M-like, there is a reason: she is one of four 4-6-2's, #3696-3699, acquired from the Delaware, Lackawanna & Western in 1943 and assigned B&M class P-5-a. These Pacifics were built by Brooks in 1924 and used primarily in passenger and milk train service on the Lackawanna's lines in Central New York State. Placed in storage in 1943, they met the needs of the B&M for serviceable steam passenger power to ease the wartime increases in passenger service. Low-drivered and fat-boilered compared to the road's own 4-6-2's, the Lackawanna's were well-liked and successful, serving the B&M until extinction in 1952. The crossing guard is at his post as the passengers relax for the three hour run to Springfield and connections south. (Donald S. Robinson)

(Above) For travelers seeking a pleasant all-day ride down the valley the train of choice was #72, the DAY WHITE MOUNTAINS EXPRESS. Leaving Berlin in the morning, it was scheduled into White River midday, with arrival at New York City via the New Haven from Springfield in the early evening. It is seen passing the lower quadrant semaphores at North Charlestown, NH behind F-3 #4227. (Donald S. Robinson)

(Above) At Claremont Junction, NH the Connecticut River Line connected with the Claremont Branch from Concord. In 1955, when Charles Ballard photographed F-2 #4224A leading Train #72 into the station, the branch had become the Claremont and Concord Railroad, and connections with New Hampshire's capital city were made with the red and silver gas-electric unit seen at the right of the station on April 2, 1955. *(Charles Ballard)*

Further south, Train #72 is crossing the steel bridge at Deerfield Junction, MA.
(Donald S. Robinson)

In its heyday the B&M operated three major routes linking Boston with Canada and Northern New England: the northernmost through Concord and Woodsville, NH; the middle through Concord and White River Junction, VT; and the southernmost, the Cheshire Branch, from a connection with the Fitchburg mainline at South Ashburnham, MA 54 miles to a connection with the Connecticut River Line at Bellows Falls, VT. At Bellows Falls the Cheshire also provided a connection with the Rutland's line from Rutland, providing a through route for freight, milk, and passenger service between Boston and Montreal and Ogdensburg, NY.

(Above) At Winchendon, MA, a few miles south of the New Hampshire line, Train #5504 is making the 8:24 AM station stop. Soon the manual gates will be dropped, and P-4-b Pacific #3715 will step out for Boston, 67.9 miles, five stops, and almost two hours distant from Winchendon.

(Donald S. Robinson)

(Opposite page, top) At Winchendon the Cheshire Branch crossed the Peterboro Branch between Worcester and Peterboro, a town in southwestern New Hampshire. Train times were coordinated to enable travelers to change trains at Winchendon. Steve Bogan caught Train #5508 behind F-2 #4255 for Boston and Train #8118 from Peterboro to Worcester behind Mogul #1487 at the Winchendon station in the summer of 1950. By the beginning of 1953 the Peterboro passenger trains were eliminated. Passenger service on the Cheshire lasted longer, until May 18, 1958, another casualty of the automobile revolution in postwar New England and the cost-cutting strategy of Patrick McGinnis. *(Steve Bogan)*

(Opposite page, bottom) The Peterboro Branch was one of the most picturesque of the B&M's fabled "Mogul Lines." Standard power was the faithful 2-6-0, as seen here at Holden, MA, eight miles north of Worcester, with down Train #8118 at 4:20 PM, August 19, 1952. *(Bob's Photos)*

In the years after World War II the Cheshire Branch had several named passenger trains, none more glamorous than its namesake train, THE CHESHIRE, with Unit #6000. Built in 1935 for the FLYING YANKEE service between Boston, Portland, and Bangor in conjunction with the Maine Central, the little streamliner's limited seating made it more suitable for the White River Junction - Boston CHESHIRE. In this Bellows Falls scene from 1950, the train has come down the Connecticut River Line from White River Junction and is completing its wying past the ball signal before proceeding east on the Cheshire Branch. The train operated with Unit #6000 from 1944 to 1952, when the equipment was reassigned to the Boston - Troy MINUTE MAN. It returned briefly in December 1956 to CHESHIRE service before its retirement in the spring of 1957.

(Donald S. Robinson)

The Cheshire

BOSTON and MAINE
RAILROAD

(Above) Bellows Falls is a small Vermont city of around 3,300 people on the Connecticut River 84 miles north of Springfield. Founded in 1753, the community has been connected with the transportation industry since the construction of the first bridge over the Connecticut and a canal around the falls were built in the late 1700's. Here the Connecticut River Line connected with the Cheshire Branch and the Rutland. To service Bellows Falls a small yard and engine facility was located just across the river at North Walpole, NH on the Cheshire. Pacific #3676, a P-2-b built in 1913, is simmering on the turntable at North Walpole in 1949 preparatory to a trip down the Cheshire.

(Charles Ballard collection)

(Below) The Connecticut River Line between East Northfield, MA and White River Junction was run as a joint operation by the Central Vermont and B&M, with sections of the line owned by each of the two roads. Central Vermont was a subsidiary of the Canadian National, and frequently operated CN units on its time freights over the CV, as shown by Canadian Locomotive Works FM C-liners #8720-8718 heading a northbound freight past the ball signal and over the Rutland diamond on October 27, 1953. *(William Brennan collection)*

Bellows Falls

The B&M under Edward S. French was an innovative company willing to invest in cutting edge technology, as shown by its early purchases of EMD freight and passenger cab units. By 1948 the road switcher concept was the newest innovation, and one that would have profound impact on the B&M and all other railroads. B&M turned a cold shoulder to the road switchers of the minor builders, Fairbanks Morse and Baldwin, but beginning in 1948 sampled products from both American Locomotive and EMD.

(Above) Alco RS-2 #1500 is on local freight ES-2 on its first revenue run at the Brightwood station in Springfield, MA. This unit was the Alco RS-2 demonstrator and lacked MU capability, limiting its use to locals and branch line operations. It was delivered in May 1948 in the switcher scheme, the only road switcher so painted, and continued to carry its Alco demo number of 1500, corresponding to the horsepower rating of this road switcher model. *(Donald S. Robinson)*

(Opposite page) The precursor to the GP-7 was EMD's unsuccessful BL-2. Looking like a cross between an F unit and a Borden's milk car, the BL-2 did not offer the visibility and operational flexibility of a true road switcher. The four B&M BL-2's, #1550-1553, were further hindered by their lack of MU capability, restricting them to commuter passenger, local freight, and switching service. All that said, the #1550 on southbound Train #236 from Portsmouth to Boston looks clean and dapper as it heads through Salisbury, MA. in the summer of 1948. At the left one of the B&M's shortest and least-remarked branches, the Amesbury Branch, joins the Eastern Route mainline. *(Donald S. Robinson)*

(Above) Arguably the best and most successful early road switcher was EMD's GP-7. EMD was late in getting off the mark on the road switcher concept, but once it did, it dominated a market first opened by Baldwin and Alco. Boston & Maine found the GP-7 a true dual service unit, good for both passenger and freight service, and purchased a total of 23 between 1950 and 1953. In this undated scene at Wakefield Junction, one of the 1950 order, #1558, heads a northbound passenger alongside beautiful Crystal Lake. The silvered trucks suggest that the scene is 1953 or later. *(Don Ball collection)*

September in Boston can be a lovely time of year, with the first hint of autumn coolness in the air. In the years following World War II it was often a time of sadness as the Red Sox once again broke the hearts of loyal New England fans, falling to the Indians in a playoff in 1948, losing to the Yankees narrowly in 1949 and again in 1950. In September 1951, when James Buckley visited North Station, the Bosox were well out of contention in third, and one could concentrate on the steam power still plentiful on the East End of the B&M.

(Above) P-2-b Pacific #3669 sports a debonair look with an Elesco feedwater heater atop its smokebox. Pacifics handled most of the commuter runs to North Shore destinations and to Reading in the early 1950's.

(James Buckley)

(Below) Pacific #3623, a P-2-a, has passed under Prison Point Bridge and is starting to accelerate out of town, laying down a perfect smoke plume in a scene repeated dozens of times per day in the final years of B&M steam.

(James Buckley)

BOSTON and MAINE
RAILROAD

(Above) By 1951 the J-1-b 3235 was the last 4-4-2 left on the roster. Assigned to commuter runs on the Central Mass Branch, the elderly Atlantic type is seen here in the neighborhood of the Boston Engine Terminal.

(James Buckley)

(Below) Consolidation #2725 appears to have picked up a little Massachusetts flora on its pilot. It is backing into the servicing area at the engine terminal. 2-8-0's performed a variety of tasks on the B&M, useful in part because the road never operated the fleet of 2-8-2's that almost every other Class I railroad did. Only the five ex-Erie Railroad N-1's leased in 1942 brought the 2-8-2 wheel arrangement to the B&M. *(James Buckley)*

BOSTON and MAINE RAILROAD
RAIL · BUS

FEBRUARY 1947

GUIDE TO BOSTON
WHERE TO GO — WHAT TO SEE — WHAT TO DO

STATE HOUSE, BOSTON

PUBLISHED MONTHLY AS A SERVICE
TO BOSTON AND MAINE PATRONS

(Above) As a terminal railroad, the B&M had a need for switch engines. It began acquiring diesel switchers in the 1930's but a number of steam switchers survived until the 1950's. Russell Munroe found the burly 631, an 0-8-0 of USRA design, at Boston on November 29, 1952. The 631 is the last of the 1922 order with American Locomotive for 22 0-8-0's, class H-2-a, rated at just over 50,000 pounds of tractive effort. *(Russell Munroe)*

(Below) At West Lynn, 0-6-0 #831 is hard at work on March 28, 1951. The engine is a former Portland Terminal unit displaced by that road's Alco switchers. The Portland Terminal was jointly owned by the B&M and the Maine Central. *(Russell Munroe)*

Steam Switchers

(Above) Also in operation that day was #451, class G-11-b.
(James Buckley)

(Below) The B&M rostered a good number of 0-6-0's, including 30 class G-11-a built in two batches in 1911 and 1913. One of the first, #401, is still busily at work on the north side of the Charles in September, 1951. Compared to the H-2's the G-11's were lightweights, capable of only around 30,000 pounds of tractive effort. (James Buckley)

(Left) Reading, 12 miles north of Boston on the Western Route, was a busy commuter terminal in the 1950's. It featured a small engine facility with turntable and water tower for the steam engines assigned to commuter runs. The water tower is shown here as it appeared on March 20, 1955. (Russell Munroe)

(Opposite page, top) Stoneham was also around 12 miles north of Boston, but northwest on the 2.4 mile Stoneham Branch that connected with the New Hampshire mainline north of Winchester. Mogul #1420 is the power for the branch's lone train to Boston on June 24, 1953. (Russell Munroe)

(Opposite page, bottom) Pacific #3622 is leaving Marblehead station on May 6, 1953. We will take a more detailed look at the Marblehead steam operations in the next pages.
(Don Ball Collection)

(Above) That same day in late March P-2-b Pacific #3662 awaits a call to return to North Station. (Russell Munroe)

North of Boston the coastline changes from the sand and bogs of the South Shore to the rocks and craggy headlands of the North. Marblehead, a little over 17 miles north of Boston, is a spot of immense beauty, a colonial town jutting out into the Atlantic, famed for sailing and its brisk salt air. Two short lines connected Marblehead to the Eastern Route main, the more direct to Boston, the Swampscott Branch, entering from the south, the other, the Salem Branch, from the west.

"We'll have to admit we're only 95% Dieselized!"

Boston and Maine Railroad

(Below) Russell Munroe knew the end of steam was near in the spring of 1956, and set out to record the final glorious season of B&M steam. Marblehead's two branches provided him with a perfect setting, as witness here P-2-b #3672 at the west end of the wye in March of that final year of steam on the B&M.

(Right) Pacifics were the usual power for the Marblehead trains. Here a P-2 is on the Salem Branch on a cool March day, with the steam plume that only winter can produce.
(Russell Munroe)

Marblehead

(Below) The 3648 is outbound at Village Street, where the tracks to Salem and Swampscott diverge. (Russell Munroe)

(Above and below) Marblehead's two lines terminated in town, requiring a wye to turn the trains. P-2-a #3654 will have the dubious honor of hauling one of the last steam-powered trains out of Marblehead later in 1956. These scenes were recorded in March of 1956. *(Both, Russell Munroe)*

(Above) Gilbert & Cole Lumber Company's red buildings provide the background for a meet of two Pacific-powered trains in March 1956. (Russell Munroe)

(Right) An outbound train on the Salem Branch is headed west near West Shore Drive behind a beetle-browed P-2 4-6-2. The Budds that are slated to replace the steamers will last a short while on the Marblehead run. Only three years remain for B&M commuter service to Marblehead, part of the rapidly declining picture for Boston-area commuter operations in the late 1950's. (Russell Munroe)

The Central Massachusetts Branch of the B&M was an east-west line built by the Boston & Lowell in the 1880's from Boston into the Connecticut River valley, connecting with the Conn River line at Northampton. Roughly parallel to and in between the Fitchburg mainline to the north and the Boston & Albany to the south, the Central Mass was not a significant through freight or passenger route. By 1956 the major business of the remaining parts of the line was the four pairs of weekday commuter trains (three from Clinton, just off the Central Mass on the Ayer-Worcester line 37 miles west of Boston, the other from Hudson, 27.7 miles out) to the metropolis.

(Left) On April 24, 1956 a Mogul has Train #3106 in tow leaving Weston for Boston. If everything is on schedule it's 8:33 AM, less than a half hour from the train's scheduled 9 AM arrival on the hour-and-a-quarter run from Clinton to North Station. (Charles Ballard)

(Above) Wayland station, at milepost 16.5, was a classic little suburban station painted in the postwar red colors.
(Don Ball collection)

(Above) On April 21, 1956, Charles and Bobbi Ballard stopped at the Clinton engine facility on their way to Boston and the April 22 last run of steam to Portland. It's hard to believe that a railroad that *TRAINS Magazine* editor David Morgan could call "New England's Most Progressive Railroad," that would replace its early FT diesels with GP-9s in just a year, could still present such a museum-like scene of branchline steam. *(Charles Ballard)*

(Right) The Ballards found a friendly reception at Clinton from yardmaster Napoleon Ouilette, posing here in the cab of 2-6-0 #1498 with Bobbi Ballard. *(Charles Ballard)*

(Below) The future on the Central Mass was also present that spring Saturday in the form of RS-2 #1534, laying over at Clinton for the weekend. By the end of the summer of 1956 steam would be gone from the branch; indeed, the entire railroad.

(Charles Ballard)

(Above) One of the most memorable steam runs on the B&M occurred on Sunday, April 22, 1956, as P-4-a 4-6-2 #3713, *The Constitution*, powered a special end of steam run from Boston to Portland and return. The big Pacific, a 1934 Lima product, is doing a photo runby on the bridge at Dover, NH. It was named after the famous warship by James S. Moore of Eastern High School in Lynn, MA as part of the 1937 naming contest. *(Charles Ballard)*

(Below and opposite page, top) Later that day the 3713 is about to leave Portland Union Station on the return run to North Station. Portland Union Station, west of the downtown section of the city, continued to serve train and bus passengers until its demolition in 1961. *(Charles Ballard)*

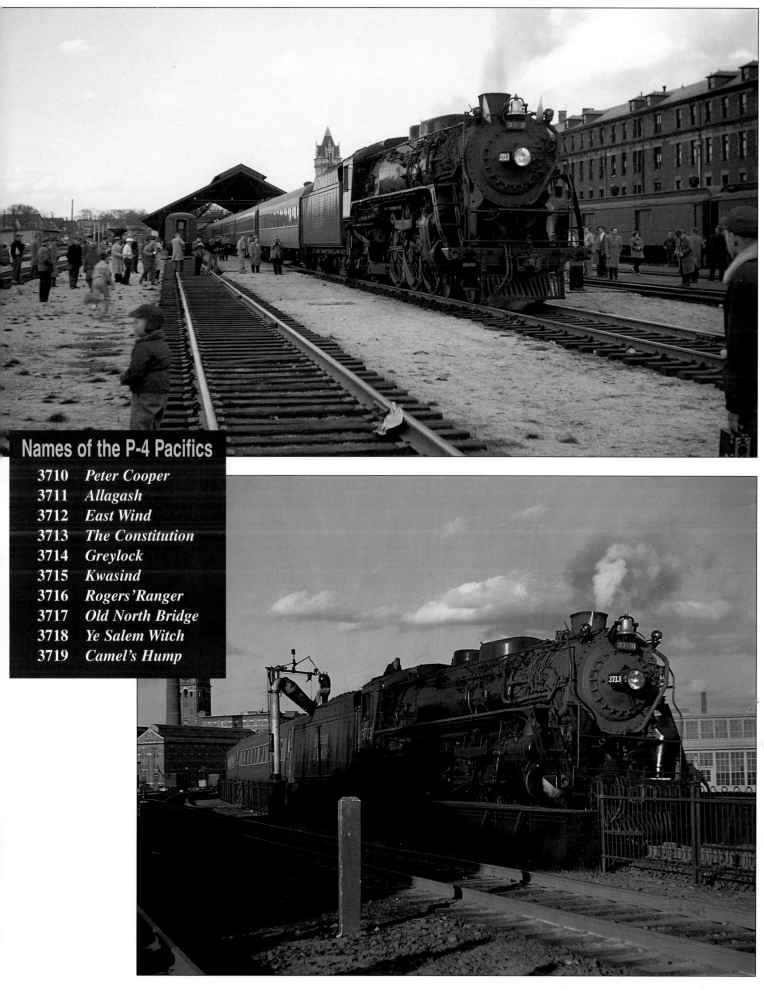

Names of the P-4 Pacifics

3710	*Peter Cooper*
3711	*Allagash*
3712	*East Wind*
3713	*The Constitution*
3714	*Greylock*
3715	*Kwasind*
3716	*Rogers'Ranger*
3717	*Old North Bridge*
3718	*Ye Salem Witch*
3719	*Camel's Hump*

(Above) Nearing the end of the day, and the end of steam on the Portland line and the B&M, the sun shines for a final time on the 3713 making a water stop in Lawrence. *(Charles Ballard)*

(Above) On July 6, 1955 Walter Zullig found Portland Terminal GP-7 #1081 ready to leave North Station on an outbound commuter run. The 1081 saw a good deal of service on the B&M from the time of its purchase in 1950 until its sale in 1956 to Maine Central, co-owner of the Portland Terminal along with the B&M. (Walter Zullig)

(Below) On April 6, 1956 the 6000 is departing North Station for Troy, 190 miles west, as Train #59, the MINUTE MAN. Travelers on the 4 hour, 15 minute ride can enjoy a meal in the buffet lounge as the 1935 vintage streamliner speeds through the hills of Massachusetts and New York State. The year 1956 will be the last for the aging equipment, ending its service on the B&M with a final stint as the CHESHIRE after being removed from the Troy run. (Charles Ballard)

North Station in the 1950's

BOSTON and MAINE RAILROAD

(Above) Alco's modern switchers never enjoyed the popularity or operational success of the first generation of Schenectady products. Model S-5, the 800 horsepower version of the 251-powered line, was especially rare, and B&M was the only New England operator of the type. S-5's #860-865 were delivered to the B&M in the Minute Man scheme in 1954 and rarely left the Boston area. The 862 was switching at North Station on July 8, 1955, at a time when silver trucks and clean maroon-and-gold paint were the order of the day. *(Walter Zullig)*

(Below) RS-2 #1532 was part of the 1949 order for steam-heater equipped units. She looks pretty with silver trucks and the big Minute Man herald on the nose heading out of Boston. The train has passed Prison Point Bridge on its run north to Lowell. *(Al Holtz)*

(Left) Still in the service it was bought to perform, the 4208 heads eastbound after crossing the Hudson River on the Fitchburg Division in 1954.

(John Bartley)

(Below) The B&M still occasionally ran two-unit, A/B sets of FT's long after it was common to see them hooked up with the F-2's. The hills of Western Massachusetts are familiar territory for the 4215 set near Greenfield on July 29, 1954. In just three years the FT's will be off the roster, replaced by the McGinnis regime's massive order of 50 EMD GP-9's in 1957. Along with the New Haven's replacement of Alco FA's in 1956, the B&M FT's will be some of the first pioneer road diesel fleets replaced, not even making the 15 years considered the norm for diesel utilization.

(Ed Kelsey)

BOSTON and MAINE RAILROAD

(Above) The 4220 set is assisted by GP-7 #1557, a 1950 EMD product, crossing the Connecticut River southbound at Holyoke. *(Walter Dance, Bob Yanosey Collection)*

(Below) Time is running out for the FT's as the 4217 rests between assignments at the Boston Engine Terminal in the summer of 1957. Like all the FT's she will be traded in on the 50 new GP-9's purchased by the road in 1957. *(Al Holtz)*

(Right) One of the changes wrought by the coming of the Budd cars was the assignment of the passenger-equipped Alco roadswitchers to other service. The 1540 and 1535, 1954-purchased RS-3's, relive some of the fun of passenger service hauling the World of Mirth circus special heading east at Concord on June 23, 1957. *(Russell Munroe)*

In many ways 1956 was the end of the old era on the B&M. Patrick McGinnis assumed the leadership of the B&M determined to change the company, at a time when many changes were inevitable. Steam had lingered on longer than many had dared to hope for, but 1956 was the last hurrah for the 2-6-0's and 4-6-2's still under steam in the Boston commuter operations, stilled by the coming of the Budd's. Although it would hang on for over a year, until January 1958, Troy service was doomed, with plans already being hatched by the tenants of Troy Union Station to eliminate all passenger service to the Collar City. The venerable Unit #6000 was taken out of service at the end of 1956. As 1956 ended and 1957 began, even more profound changes were beginning. The order for the 50 new GP-9's was placed, with the FT's put on the block as trade-in's. A new color scheme (really a series of schemes) using blue/black/white, colors with no tradition on the historically maroon B&M, was introduced, in patterns glaringly modern and reminiscent of the similarly modern McGinnis schemes imposed on the New Haven during McGinnis's short stay there. The GP-9's and the Fairbanks-Morse Talgo set in the new blue and black colors presented a shocking break from the tradition, along with the replacement of the Minute Man with the large BM logo. More than anything else, a spirit of disillusionment permeated the B&M in 1957: fear of what the future held, a sense that the automobile and the truck held the upper hand in transportation in Northern New England, a concern for the long-term financial viability of the company.

(Below) By July of 1957 the transition from locomotive-hauled trains to Budds was well underway. The 1956 order of 34 additional Budd units, including 30 RDC-9's — the so-called "Half Budds" with only one prime mover — allowed the road to operate multiple-unit trains of Budds economically. Al Holtz found an elevated vantage point to capture this view of three units leaving Tower A behind on an outbound run. *(Al Holtz)*

1957

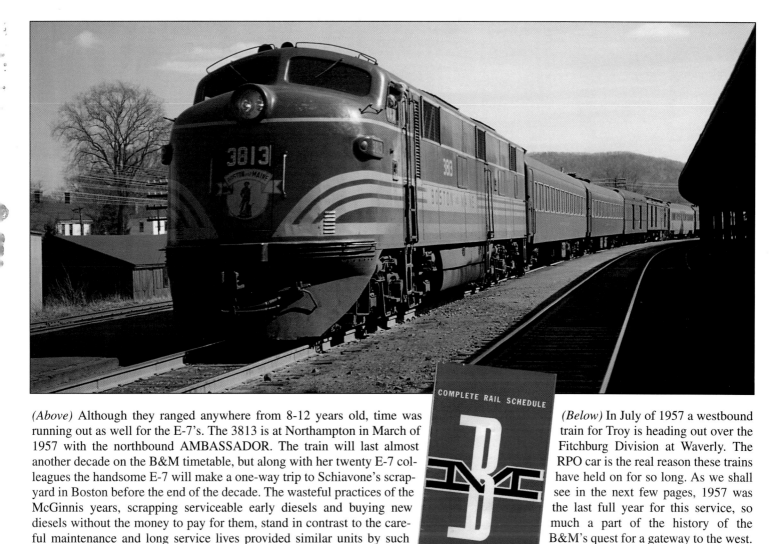

(Above) Although they ranged anywhere from 8-12 years old, time was running out as well for the E-7's. The 3813 is at Northampton in March of 1957 with the northbound AMBASSADOR. The train will last almost another decade on the B&M timetable, but along with her twenty E-7 colleagues the handsome E-7 will make a one-way trip to Schiavone's scrapyard in Boston before the end of the decade. The wasteful practices of the McGinnis years, scrapping serviceable early diesels and buying new diesels without the money to pay for them, stand in contrast to the careful maintenance and long service lives provided similar units by such roads as the Bangor & Aroostook and Seaboard. (Al Holtz)

COMPLETE RAIL SCHEDULE

B
M

BOSTON AND MAINE RAILROAD

JULY 8, 1956
DAYLIGHT SAVING TIME

(Below) In July of 1957 a westbound train for Troy is heading out over the Fitchburg Division at Waverly. The RPO car is the real reason these trains have held on for so long. As we shall see in the next few pages, 1957 was the last full year for this service, so much a part of the history of the B&M's quest for a gateway to the west. (Al Holtz)

End of the Troy Trains

By 1957 it was clear that the B&M's east-west passenger service, Boston to Troy, was on its last legs. The New York Central was always the route of choice for Bostonians heading west on the rails. The Troy trains on the Fitchburg line relied on mail and local service in a sparsely populated corridor too far from the large cities of the region to build up much patronage. Postwar service on the route was still regular enough to sustain the Minute Man on a daily basis, with four other pairs of trains Monday through Saturday and two on Sunday. But competition from automobiles was relentless, and the McGinnis administration was anxious to cut costs from underpatronized passenger service. The decision was made in 1957 to close Troy Union Station at the beginning of the new year, ending the need for Troy-Albany service on the New York Central. The D&H's pair of New York-Montreal trains, the daytime LAURENTIANS and overnight MONTREAL LIMITEDS were rerouted via Albany Union Station. For the B&M, it meant the end of passenger service beyond Fitchburg on the east-west main. On January 18, 1958, the last B&M train for Boston left the Troy Union Station, ending passenger service in a city that once hosted name trains of four major railroads. Later that year the great structure was razed. Credit Charles Ballard with the foresight to record in color the last months of this service.

(*Above*) Budd cars, such as the single unit on eastbound Train #58 at Hoosick, NY seen from the Route 7 overpass, handled many of the Troy trains during the McGinnis years as ridership faded and the management put more and more emphasis on saving money. Note the three different spellings: Hoosac Tunnel; the Hoosic River; and the towns in New York, Hoosick with a final "k." The separation of the two mainline tracks is evident at this spot. Two miles to the east at Petersburgh Junction the B&M crossed at grade until its abandonment in 1953 the "Corkscrew Division" of the Rutland that followed the flood-prone valley of the Little Hoosic from Bennington to a connection with the Boston & Albany at Chatham, NY. The date of this shot is October 13, 1957. (*Charles Ballard*)

(*Below*) The largest town along the Hoosic in New York is Hoosick Falls. On a sparkling October 20, 1957 Train #68 is eastbound along the Hoosic east of the village center led by B&M's only E-8, #3821. By this time almost nothing remained to suggest that Hoosick Falls had once been a major industrial center. From 1852 to 1924 the Walter A. Wood Mowing and Reaping Machine Company, the largest farm machinery builder in the East, had built farm machinery at a sprawling 85 acre factory complex alongside the river. The factory had seven miles of railroad tracks and kept two switch crews busy. Wood died in 1892, and his successors failed to anticipate the transformation of farming occasioned by self-propelled equipment. The Wood company went on building only horsedrawn equipment until its inevitable demise in 1924. For a time the Wood mansion was used as the town's high school, but in the 1960's was demolished in favor of a new building, the last reminder of a vanished industrial empire. The 3821, by the way, will avoid the fate of the 21 older E-7's scrapped in the late 1950's. It will be sold to the Missouri Pacific, where it will be renumbered as that road's #42. (*Charles Ballard*)

(Above) Between the Vermont/Massachusetts state line and Johnsonville the eastbound and westbound tracks follow separate rights of way as much as one-half mile apart. The Troy and Boston and the Albany Northern had both built east from the Hudson Valley in the 1850's, aiming for the Hoosac Tunnel and the low-grade route to New England. The delay in finishing the tunnel spelled doom for the Albany Northern, which was abandoned in 1860. Nineteen years later, after completion of the tunnel, the Boston, Hoosac Tunnel and Western utilized the abandoned right of way as far as Johnsonville. Both lines were acquired by the Fitchburg and became part of the B&M in 1900, making a double track line out of two formerly separate rights of way. At Hoosick Falls the eastbound track crossed under the westbound, with left-hand running to Johnsonville. On January 4, 1958 Train #51 is westbound for Troy at the East Buskirk station behind E-7 #3809. (Charles Ballard)

(Right) On January 5, 1958 Sunday-only Train #67 is passing East Buskirk enroute to Troy Union Station and connections to Albany and points west. Arriving at Troy at 1:45, the train will be turned and return to Boston as #68 with a 3 PM departure time from Troy.
(Charles Ballard)

(Above) Buskirk station at one time served eastbound passengers, but by January 5, 1958 Train #58's two Budd cars were not scheduled to pause on their way to Boston. Buskirk and East Buskirk stations were about one-half mile apart, with a single station agent working both locations, traveling to East Buskirk as needed from the Buskirk station alongside Route 67. At Eagle Bridge the river loops away to the north, and the Johnsonville Dam downstream creates a large reservoir for the seven miles between Johnsonville and Buskirk. The eastbound line stayed close to the river while the westbound pursued a more direct route, rejoining it between Johnsonville and Valley Falls. *(Charles Ballard)*

(Below) Further west Train #67 on January 12, 1958 is just east of Johnsonville, the junction of the freight mainline to Mechanicville and Rotterdam Junction and the passenger line to Troy. *(Charles Ballard)*

(Above) Maroon E-7 #3802 pauses at the Johnsonville station with Train #51 on January 15, 1958. This train was an all-stops local that left Boston in the early morning hours and arrived at Troy around 8:45 in the morning. Johnsonville had once hosted not only the B&M but the shortline Greenwich and Johnsonville, which headed north over the Hoosic River to its namesake town in Washington County and a connection with the D&H's Washington Branch at Salem Junction. By this time the Greenwich to Johnsonville line of the G&J had long been abandoned, but the rest of the line has persevered, first as a subsidiary of the D&H, and now as the Battenkill Railroad.

(Charles Ballard)

(Below) At Johnsonville the Troy Branch diverged from the freight mainline and headed southwest for 16 miles to its namesake city. Both lines passed through the village of Valley Falls, the freight line alongside the river and the Troy Branch a mile to the south. At the Valley Falls station on October 13, 1957 Train #58, the Sunday BERKSHIRE, passes on its trip to Boston. Budd #6155 has the honors on this beautiful autumn day that promises glorious fall colors for the few passengers on the ride up through the Hoosic Valley and over the Berkshires.

(Charles Ballard)

Troy Branch

(Above) Troy is a hilly city aligned on a north-south axis along the Hudson. To leave the river valley eastbound required the B&M to climb gradually through the Lansingburgh section of Troy. Lansingburgh, also called North Troy, was a pleasant residential area of single-family homes and small neighborhood shopping areas, seen here as the backdrop for Train #68, the TACONIC, beginning its four and a half hour trip to Boston a few minutes after 3 PM on October 13, 1957. *(Charles Ballard)*

(Below) Another shot of the 3809 on January 5, 1958 finds the westbound train passing under the covered bridge in North Troy near Oakwood Cemetary. Built in 1885, the structure fell victim to arsonists in 1963. *(James Odell Collection)*

(Above) That same sunny afternoon Mr. Ballard lensed the B&M's Rensselaer Street Yard and engine facility in North Troy. At this spot in 1850 ground was broken for the Troy and Boston by a group of notables including Troy's hero of the Mexican War, General John Wool. The North Troy yard was one of two in the city used by the road, the Adams Street yard in South Troy serving the industries in that part of the city and a connection with the New York Central. *(Charles Ballard)*

(Above) Troy Union Station was built in 1902 by the New York Central. It was a Beaux Arts masterpiece in the grand Vanderbilt style, designed by the architectural firm of Reed and Stern, which followed the Troy project with New York City's Grand Central Station. The station anchored downtown Troy and provided travelers with frequent schedules for Albany via the New York Central, points north via the D&H in New York State and the Rutland in Vermont, and east on the B&M. Its end in 1958 underlined the decline of Troy, a once-proud industrial and transportation center that at the time was one of the largest American cities left without rail passenger service. By 1957 the Budd cars were assuming more and more of the passenger assignments. Budd #6155 is at Troy Union Station on October 10, 1957, preparing to leave the six-track terminal for points east. *(Charles Ballard)*

(Left) Downtown Troy was a maze of tracks leading in and out of the station area. Towers 1 and 2 spanned the tracks and controlled the interlocking plants around the station. The B&M ran up 6th Street leaving the station, as shown here by Train #58 leaving town on October 10, 1957.

(Charles Ballard)

(Below) On January 22, 1956, R-1 Mountain #4113, *Black Arrow*, is in stationary heating service at Mechanicville. One of 18 4-8-2's purchased from Baldwin, she will be the last of her type on the B&M, going to scrap in September, 1956. The first 13 of the series, #4100-4112, were sold to the Baltimore & Ohio in the summer of 1947, where they stayed in use until 1957. The R-1 was the apotheosis of steam freight power on the B&M, and its design was copied during World War II by the Lehigh & Hudson River. *(Charles Ballard)*

York County in Southern Maine is well-known to readers of Kenneth Roberts, perhaps America's finest historical novelist. The simple life of the Southern Maine coast described by Roberts changed forever when the predecessor rail lines of the B&M arrived in the 1840's. After years of intense competition between the B&M and the Eastern Railroad which had led to the building of parallel competing lines up the coastline to Portland the absorption of the Eastern by the B&M led eventually to the exclusive privilege of linking the Pine Tree State to the rest of the nation's rail system. The Western Route of the Portland Division provided a direct route for trains heading from Maine to Boston or west at Lowell Junction to the Fitchburg mainline for service to Mechanicville or Worcester via Ayer.

(Above) In June of 1960 E-7's #3809-3808 are on the point of a Boston-bound passenger train from Portland at the Kennebunk station. Time is running out for locomotive-drawn passenger trains to Portland, and for the E-7's that pull them.

(Russell Munroe)

(Below) The overhead shot of the 3808-3809 at Kennebunk gives an indication of how long these twin-engined EMD units were. The view down the tracks shows the long straight section of right-of-way characteristic of coastal Southern Maine.

(Russell Munroe)

Maine

(Right) RS-3 #1508 leads a west-bound freight through Kennebunk on February 7, 1960. One of the 1954 order of RS-3's, the 1508 features the Minute Man emblem under each cab window instead of on the front (long hood), and the angled number boards and double sealed-beam headlights of the later RS-3's. *(Russell Munroe)*

(Right) F-2 #4261 heads a south-bound at Arundel in the spring of 1960. *(Russell Munroe)*

(Below) The Portland run afforded high-speed running in Southern Maine. This shot of a northbound at Arundel in 1960 suggests speed! The 3809-3808 pair are once again in charge.
(Russell Munroe)

(Left) By the late 1950's rail passenger service was declining quickly. To cut costs and attract passengers back to the rails, some executives thought that lightweight trains were the answer, the equivalent of the streamliner revolution in the 1930's. Pat McGinnis was a believer, and so both the New Haven and the B&M invested in lightweight trains. Fortunately for the B&M, its investment was modest, limited to the Fairbanks-Morse powered Talgo train delivered around the beginning of 1958. The Talgo, based on a Spanish design, was powered by two P-12-42 power units, one on each end, numbered 1-2. Five sets of three connected, low-slung cars completed the train. Intended for the ailing Boston-Portland market, the train was too little, too late, and in the minds of many, too bizarre with its wild McGinnis paint scheme of triangles and checkerboards. It finished a short (but compared to other lightweights, respectable) service life on Eastern Route commuter runs, as shown here at Newburyport crossing the blue waters of the Merrimack in August, 1961.

(Russell Munroe)

Talgo

The Talgo was still going strong in 1964, seen here crossing at Salem in June of that year.
(Russell Munroe)

(Above) With the retirement of the E-7's most of the remnants of B&M's intercity passenger service was entrusted to the Budd "Highliners." From Boston in the late 1950's and early 1960's one could travel via the Highliners to Portland, North Conway, Montreal, Berlin, White River Junction. One of the more interesting Budd routes was Boston-Montreal in cooperation with Canadian Pacific. At Wells River, VT Train #32 is Boston-bound behind Budds of each cooperating railroad. The lead unit, #6205, provides the baggage space for the passengers now routed to Boston through White River Junction and the New Hampshire mainline rather than the old route of the CP trains over the White Mountains Line through Woodsville and Plymouth. *(Walter Zullig)*

(Below) The Portland trains lingered on until 1964. On February 15, 1964 a north-bound Highliner pauses at the handsome station at Exeter, New Hampshire.

(Russell Munroe)

Highliners

(Above) The one-of-a-kind 1500 was a regular on the Peterboro Branch. On Christmas Eve of 1962 the RS-2 is heading the local freight at Winchendon. It looks like 1962 will be a White Christmas in the hills of Massachusetts and New Hampshire.
(Russell Munroe)

(Above) Alco roadswitchers were popular in New England. All the major New England roads except BAR relied heavily on the RS-2 and RS-3 to handle a variety of tasks, from local freight to commuter service to road freights. Once the B&M's fleet of Budd cars was in place the versatile RS's roamed the system, handling all sorts of assignments. B&M #1530 was a 1949-built RS-2. As delivered it was equipped with a steam generator for passenger service, but by August 7, 1960, when Russell Munroe found it at Lincoln, NH, it was in its normal working environment. Lincoln is a paper and logging town deep in the heart of New Hampshire's White Mountains, the northern terminus of the Pemigewasset Valley Branch. The "Pemi" left the Woodsville-Concord Lakes Region Line at Plymouth (the route of the ALOUETTE and RED WING until the northern part was abandoned in 1954) to reach Lincoln. The branch provided decent traffic for the B&M until 1970, when the paper mill at Lincoln closed.
(Russell Munroe)

BOSTON AND MAINE RAILROAD

TIME TABLE No. 2

SUPERSEDING TIME TABLE NO. 1

FOR EMPLOYEES ONLY

EFFECTIVE 12.01 AM SUNDAY

APRIL 28, 1963

EASTERN STANDARD TIME

STUDY THE SPECIAL INSTRUCTIONS AND NOTE ALL CHANGES

(*Above and below*) RS-3's were the usual power for local freights on the Eastern Route to Salem. RS-3 #1509 is at Swampscott, while the 1518 is on the trestle at Oak Island, Revere, both shot in July, 1964. *(Both, Russell Munroe)*

(Above) The late afternoon was a busy time at the joint Central Vermont-B&M station at White River Junction. The southbound and northbound AMBASSADORS met here around 4 PM, with power exchanged between the two roads. Trains #31-32, remnants of the Montreal-Boston service via the Canadian Pacific, connected around this time also before their termination in January 1965, providing passengers the option of traveling north up the river to Wells River, St. Johnsbury or Newport, and down to Boston over the New Hampshire mainline. *(Walter Zullig)*

(Above) The passenger rush over, a Boston-bound freight behind the 4228 A/B and the 4258 heads out of the yard on the south side of town and over the bridge to the Granite State on the New Hampshire mainline. *(Walter Zullig)*

(Above and below) Shiny CV GP-9 #4928 is preparing the northbound AMBASSADOR — just an RPO and a single coach — for departure. The CV's Alco S-4 switcher #8162 has backed the B&M power set, #4227A/B, and the southbound into the station for the 4:15 departure for Springfield and Gotham. *(Both, William J. Brennan)*

Connecticut River Line

(Above) The decision of the McGinnis administration to use Budds for all local and commuter passenger service out of North Station released the RS-3's for freight service. The favored assignments for the "tubs" as they were affectionately known was local service around Boston, and road service on the Conn River Line. Phase III RS-3 #1517, the final unit of the 1954 RS-3 order, leads two F booster units on a typical Conn River lashup south of Bellows Falls in the early spring of 1964.

(Steve Bogan)

(Right) The six GP-18's purchased in 1961 were the first low-nosed units on the road and for a decade the newest road power. Usually associated with trains on the East-West Line, the 1753 is leading a train north through Bellows Falls in 1962, its McGinnis scheme gleaming in the low late-afternoon sun.

(Jim Shaughnessy)

(Above) Railfans in search of first-generation lashups in the 1960's learned quickly that the Connecticut River Line was the best place to find RS-3's and F-units. Train JS-2 was a dependable daylight southbound, seen here at Greenfield in November 1962. *(Bob's Photo)*

(Below) Long after regular passenger assignments were gone for the RS-3's they still came in handy on occasion for passenger extras. The B&M's last new RS-3, #1519, is sporting the blue dip paint scheme on May 29, 1967 bringing the Ringling Brothers/Barnum & Bailey circus train south through Claremont Junction, NH. *(Donald S. Robinson)*

Through the 1950's and on into the early 1960's long-distance passenger service on the B&M continued to decline. The Troy trains disappeared in early 1958, Boston-Bangor service in 1960, and Portland service in 1964, leaving the Pine Tree State virtually bereft of passenger service. "Real" trains of locomotives pulling cars, such as the ALOUETTE and White River Junction - Boston service, were replaced by Budd cars serving the last remaining patrons. The last chapter of long-distance service in Northern New England before Amtrak was written by the Washington-New York-Montreal trains run cooperatively by the Pennsylvania, New Haven, B&M, Central Vermont, and Canadian National. Two pairs of trains lasted until 1966: #75-76, the daytime AMBASSADORS, and #20-21, the overnight northbound MONTREALER and southbound WASHINGTONIAN. The little trains attracted rail photographers from all over anxious to record the end of an era in travel that had begun a century and a quarter earlier.

(Right) The AMBASSADOR's roll sign at Grand Central Station, New York, beckons. With ten scheduled stops on the B&M portion of the run between Springfield and White River, the grandly named AMBASSADOR was really a local dependent on its mail contract to remain viable. The night trains operated via Penn Station for direct service to Washington via the Pennsy. *(William J. Brennan)*

(Below) At Holyoke the B&M crosses and parallels the broad Connecticut River. The northbound AMBASSADOR this June 1966 day is led by passenger phase IV F-3 #4227 and RS-3 #1507. The lead unit was a regular on this run throughout its tenure on the road. This overhead view shows the mesh-covered rectangular dynamic brake grids that help to distinguish later F-3s such as #4227 (often called F-5s) from the otherwise similar F-7, which has a circular dynamic brake fan in place of the mesh grids. *(William J. Brennan)*

The Ambassador

(Above) The 1949 order of F-7's also appeared on the AMBASSADOR. F-7 #4265A-B is having no problem moving the Canadian National RPO and two coaches north through Greenfield in the last days of service in the summer of 1966. (William J. Brennan)

(Left) The 4227 was a solid performer but a bit ragged in appearance in the 1960's. Comparing the engineer's-side profile with the preceding fireman's-side shot shows the unusual "gray" stripe, really just a curious shedding of the imitation-gold striping to reveal the primer below. The cash-poor condition of the road after the McGinnis takeover was nowhere more obvious than the deteriorating paint on the older maroon units. This is southbound Train #76 near Putney, VT on June 19, 1965. (George Berisso)

Springfield

Springfield is the largest Massachusetts city in the Connecticut Valley region. It was an important railroad junction, with the Connecticut River Line of the B&M forming a north-south link in the valley with the New Haven's line up from Hartford and New Haven and crossing the east-west Boston & Albany mainline of the New York Central west of the Union Station that served all three roads.

(Above) A number of photographers shot the daytime AMBASSADORS but far fewer shot the overnight trains, the northbound MONTREALER and southbound WASHINGTONIAN. Phase IV F-3 #4228 and GP-7 #1555 are the power for the up train, resting in the engine terminal near the station shared by the B&M and New Haven on a June evening close to the end of service in 1966. *(William J. Brennan)*

(Below) The 4228's headlight is on and the train begins its northward trek to the metropolis on the St. Lawrence. Notice the healthy 7-car consist for the night train, a sharp contrast to the 2-4 cars normal for the AMBASSADORS in the last years. The McGinnis scheme hasn't worn too well — the paint is flaking and fading on the F unit. *(William J. Brennan)*

(Above) The southbound AMBASSADOR has completed the B&M portion of its run from White River Junction and is backing into the station on the New Haven's connecting track. The diamonds in the foreground are the crossing with the B&A. The contrast in paint schemes between the two units shows the total change of image wrought by McGinnis. *(T. J. McNamara)*

(Below) After elimination of passenger service on the B&M in 1966, Springfield still saw cab units on Connecticut River Line freights. The 4265, one of the F-7's, is at the head of a three unit consist of old timers, F-7 A/B and RS-3, seen from the New Haven tower. *(Jonathan Plant)*

(Above) Russell Munroe found the 4266A about to depart Berlin yard for White River Junction on the short afternoon of February 29, 1964. The 100 mile line from the Conn River Line at Wells River to Berlin enjoyed a healthy freight business well into the 1970's and 1980's due to the paper industry in Berlin. *(Russell Munroe)*

(Above) Southbound train UJ-2 is on the roll out of the White Mountains at Gorham on June 13, 1967 behind two GP-9's.
(Donald S. Robinson)

(Below) Groveton, NH is the northernmost location reached by B&M on its own trackage, and an interchange point with the main-line of the Grand Trunk. GP-7 #1536 is switching the industries of Groveton on June 13, 1967. *(Donald S. Robinson)*

(Left and below) By 1967 only two ball signals remained on the B&M, at Waumbek Junction and Whitefield, NH. Local G-1 passed both on its return to Whitefield and Littleton on June 13, 1967. *(Both, Donald S. Robinson)*

The White Mountains are in the distance as UJ-2 passes Lisbon, NH in the evening of July 26, 1966. UJ-2 was scheduled out of Berlin late in the afternoon, making the long days of summer the only feasible time to chase the train along the scenic Berlin line.
(Donald S. Robinson)

The B&M was a terminal railroad, and not surprisingly found it useful to employ a large number of end-cab diesel switchers. Hardly any visit to B&M tracks did not include a sighting of one of the many little mules on their appointed rounds. Let's take a look at a sampling of the B&M's switcher fleet in action in the 1960's and early 1970's.

(Left) Among the smallest of the B&M's switchers were the 10 General Electric 44-tonners, #110-119, purchased between 1940 and 1948. The second to the last purchased, #118, was switching the Rutland diamond at Bellows Falls on August 24, 1964.

(J. W. Swanberg)

(Above) In the same vicinity Alco #1188, the last of a 16-unit order of 660 horsepower S-3's, is moving Steamtown's #89 over the Connecticut River Bridge between Bellows Falls and North Walpole on May 1, 1964. *(Matthew Herson)*

(Below) The B&M owned 24 of the useful little EMD SW-1's. The 1118 at the Boston Engine Terminal on December 17, 1967 was purchased in 1949. *(Matthew Herson Collection)*

Switchers

(Right) The B&M's "Four Aces," #1111, is another SW-1, purchased in 1939 and still going strong in its original scheme, reminiscent of steam engine tenders. It's seen at the Boston Engine Terminal on October 14, 1958.
(Bill Volkmer Collection)

(Above) The #1271 is a relatively muscular switcher, one of the 1,000 horsepower Alco S-4's purchased in 1950. She is on a local passing by the station site at Greenfield in 1966.
(William J. Brennan)

(Right) The Minute Man maroon scheme looked very nice on end cab switchers such as SW-9 #1224 on a local at Watertown, MA in 1971.
(Bob Yanosey Collection)

(Left, top and center) Johnsonville, NY was once a major junction on the B&M. At this small town in northern Rensselaer County the double-track Troy Branch — the original Fitchburg Railroad mainline into New York State and the route of the Boston-Troy passenger service until its termination in January 1958 — left the mainline for the 16 mile run to the Collar City. In these shots from the summer of 1967 the large brick tower that once controlled the movements through the junction stands unused and abandoned; the branch itself is little more than a streak of rust. The angled highway bridge carried Route 67 over the tracks of the branch, affording a good position to shoot westbounds. The station retains its B&M colors but is about to be refurbished as a private dwelling. At one time, shortline Greenwich & Johnsonville entered town from the north, but this line has long been abandoned leaving the D&H controlled shortline dependent on its connection to the Washington Branch of its owner for a connection to the outside world.
(Both, Jeremy Plant)

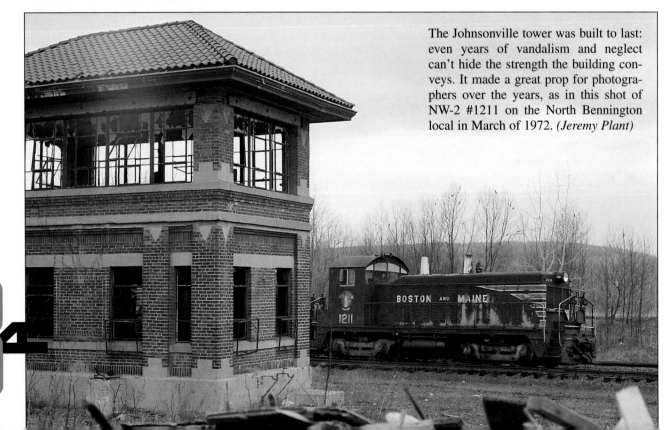

The Johnsonville tower was built to last: even years of vandalism and neglect can't hide the strength the building conveys. It made a great prop for photographers over the years, as in this shot of NW-2 #1211 on the North Bennington local in March of 1972. *(Jeremy Plant)*

Johnsonville

Troy was the largest community in New York State served by the B&M. By the late 1800's it was a major industrial city, with a large steel mill, iron foundries, shirt and collar factories, breweries, and food processing companies. It was also the retail center for the counties east of the Hudson, all the way to the state border with Vermont and Massachusetts. This Hudson River city, with a population of around 100,000 in the early decades of the century, suffered a precipitous decline in the postwar period, as industry moved to the South and city dwellers discovered the suburbs. After the closing of Union Station in 1958 passenger service to Troy, once available on four railroads, disappeared; freight service to the B&M's small yard in North Troy from Mechanicville continued until 1971, but was barely a shadow of the traffic once handled on the branch.

(Above) GP-9 #1730 is on the point of an eight-car Troy local between Valley Falls and Johnsonville about 10:00 AM in early April 1968, heading slowly upgrade about two miles from the junction with the branch. *(Jeremy Plant)*

(Below) The junction was not set up to allow trains from Mechanicville to proceed directly down the branch. The Geep has run around the train and is hauling it caboose-first about 10 mph down the former high-speed passenger line.

(Jeremy Plant)

End of the Troy Branch

In 1967 an exciting new service was inaugurated jointly by B&M and the New York Central. Unit coal trains originating on the Pittsburgh and Lake Erie destined for the Public Service Company of New Hampshire electric generating facility in Bow, NH (near Concord) began operation. In the years since then, unit coal trains to Bow, and later to Mt. Tom, MA have added a good deal of variety to railfanning along the B&M, not to mention the healthy boost they have given to the B&M's finances.

(Above) On a cold, clear, cloudless and snowless December 27, 1967, a sextet of Geeps from B&M, NYC, and P&LE team up to power the Bow coal train over the Hudson. *(Jeremy Plant)*

(Below) By 1968 the B&M's partner in the Bow venture had become Penn Central, and the mixture of engines trailing Bluebird #1745 at Valley Falls, NY with a westbound train of empties reflects the change: a former NYC U-30B, PRR GP-35, and P&LE GP-9. The winter of 1967-68 was apparently a light year for snowfall along the valley of the Hoosic, as this time of year, March, still usually sees snow covering the ground. *(Jeremy Plant)*

Bow Coal Trains

(Above) Penn Central power predominated on the Bow trains in the early 1970's, but occasionally an all-B&M consist showed up. On September 11, 1972, GP-9 #1720 leads two mates into the yard at North Adams with westbound empties bound for the P&LE. *(Jack Armstong)*

(Below) Penn Central's engine of choice for coal train service was the GP38-2, so it was not surprising to find two of these units bracketing two Bluebirds around noontime of a fine, early September day in 1974. The train is on the busy joint D&H/B&M line between Crescent and Mechanicville, hurrying into the yard about five miles away to get out of the way of the ADIRONDACKS and the numerous freights of both lines that usually appeared in the afternoon hours.

(Jeremy Plant)

From bridge level the 1742 heads the usual four unit set of GP-9's westbound into Mechanicville. The train will take a sharp turn to the south at the end of the bridge approach and pass the former junction with the shortline Saratoga & Schuylerville, a one-time B&M branch.

(Jim Shaughnessy)

Along with Hoosac Tunnel the photographic highlight of the West End was the bridge over the Hudson just north of Mechanicville. Between 1957 and the purchase of the GP-38-2's in 1973 the chances were good that you would see four of five Geeps on each freight, but the bridge afforded good shots from any number of different angles, keeping things interesting.

(Below) Walter Zullig found a spot on the east bank of the Hudson to record an eastbound led by one of the GP-18's crossing the bridge on November 4, 1968. *(Walter Zullig)*

(Above) The Hudson flows almost due north and south in this part of New York State. Looking north, we see a five unit set heading west, shot from a convenient parking spot off U. S. Route 4 at Riverside. The train is leaving Rensselaer County, which it entered at Petersburgh Junction at the Vermont border, and is entering Saratoga County. At this point the waters of the Hudson provide the route of the Champlain Canal connecting New York with the St. Lawrence via Lake Champlain. *(Jim Shaughnessy)*

(Below) The sharp curves at each approach to the bridge were prone to derailments that could disable the West End mainline. The problem was acute in the desperate years of 1970 and 1971 when cash for maintenance was in short supply and track conditions were at an all-time low. On June 6, 1971 the wreck crew is rerailing GP-9 #1711, a trailing unit on a westbound that derailed approaching the bridge. *(Jim Shaughnessy)*

The Boston & Maine's aspirations to be more than a regional or terminal New England railroad have always been linked to the Hoosac Tunnel: a virtually gradeless path through the mountains separating New England from New York State and the West. Canal builders first dreamed of penetrating Hoosac Mountain and connecting the watersheds of the Connecticut and Hudson Rivers. With the building of the Western Railroad from Boston to Albany in the 1840's over the Berkshire grades, the Tunnel project gained new credibility as a low grade rail alternative to the B & A. Brokered by Massachusetts business and political leaders, the Tunnel took almost twenty years to complete (with a seven-year hiatus in the middle). Before light shone through the 25,081 feet separating the east and west portals in 1875, 195 workers had died and $14 million had been expended.

Was it worth it? The bore links the valleys of the Deerfield and Hoosic Rivers, giving the road an easy crossing of the mountains. Electrification in 1919-11 permitted electric engines to take over from steam in the 20 minute, 7.9 mile trip from North Adams to East Portal (the village of Hoosac Tunnel).

Dieselization in 1946 banished both steam and electrics from the Bore, which in the busy wartime years carried over 40 trains a day, down to a still-respectable 14 or so in the 1960's. The Fitchburg Division was the key to the success of the road as it tried to maintain some semblance of long-distance freight service, and the Tunnel the key to the competitive advantage the B&M had over its competitors.

(Above) On October 18, 1969, the Massachusetts Bay Railroad Enthusiasts sponsored a trip from North Station to Rotterdam Junction and return — the entire east-west railroad. RDC #6155 led seven other units — the 6907, 6903, 6123, 6301, 6927, 6924, and 6153 — on this epic foliage trip, seen here westbound coming up the Deerfield River valley east of the tunnel. *(Jeffrey Plant)*

(Above and below) Your authors happened to be in the vicinity of Hoosac Tunnel that day. As might be expected, the Special complicated train movements on the West End. After its departure, GP-18 #1753 followed on the point of a heavy westbound freight, succeeded shortly afterward by an eastbound behind the 1751. It was a glorious fall day in the Massachusetts mountains, the last day of B&M railfanning for Jeremy Plant before induction into the Army two days later. *(Jeffrey/Jeremy Plant)*

The 14 NW-2's in the 1200 series were jacks of all trades on the B&M. The NW-2 was marketed by EMD before World War II as its "big" end-cab switcher. With 1,000 horsepower and MU connections the tough little mules were ubiquitous around Mechanicville, switching the yard, working the hump, heading off individually or in pairs on locals west to Scotia and Rotterdam Junction and east to North Bennington and North Adams. With the first dating back to 1941, before even the first FTs, the NW-2 was one of the best investments the road ever made.

(Above) Two of the four MU-equipped 1200's, #1210-1213, have no trouble moving a heavy ME-4 under the signal bridge at Eagle Bridge. The train is running on the westbound main to allow it to diverge at Hoosick Junction and head up the North Bennington Branch. It's March of 1972. *(Jeremy Plant)*

(Below) A few days after Christmas in 1970 the 1210 and 1212 are enroute to Rotterdam Junction at the Coons crossings, just west of the Mechanicville yard limits. The local will work the industries of Scotia and the Scotia Naval Depot on its way to the Penn Central interchange. *(Jeremy Plant)*

NW-2's

(Above) On a sunny but blustery November day in 1970 the 1210 and 1213 are doing flat switching in the Mechanicville Yard. The string of cars in the background is in the separate and parallel D&H yard. Despite their seedy appearance, NW-2's just last and last and last — they have another decade of service ahead before retirement in the early 1980's. *(Jeffrey Plant)*

(Below) The original NW-2, #1200, is the Mechanicville hump engine on October 12, 1963. She is strutting her stuff in front of railfans treated to a tour of the yard in conjunction with the founding of the Mohawk & Hudson Chapter of the National Railway Historical Society. *(Charles Ballard)*

On February 21, 1970, Budds 6207-6136-6306-6126-6112-6135 made the trip up from Boston on an RRE excursion. The cars are positioned nicely to show the station at North Conway.

(J. W. Swanberg)

Downhill skiing emerged as a popular recreational activity in Northern New England in the years before World War II and burgeoned in the years after the war. The most direct route to the ski slopes of New Hampshire's White Mountains was via the Conway Branch, which left the Boston-Portland mainline at Rollinsford, NH for the additional 70 mile trek to the mountains. Regular passenger service to North Conway ended in 1961, but the wintertime excursion trains continued on into the 1970's.

(Below) On February 26, 1972, the final B&M excursion train to North Conway needed GP-18 #1751 and GP-9 #1730 to escort the Budds through the heavy blizzard-like conditions. Budds were too light to safely buck buildups of ice and snow at grade crossings, making the use of diesel locomotives imperative in conditions such as this. *(James Herold, Bob Wilt collection)*

Conway Branch

(Above) A maroon F-7 on the point of a freight in 1971 was fairly commonplace on the Conn River Line but a distinct rarity on the east-west mainlines. It was enough of a prize to tempt your authors to embark on a perilous chase over the snow-covered roads of Rensselaer County in pursuit of this eastbound, seen here at the eastbound departure yard in Mechanicville, only to end up ignominiously in a ditch in Johnsonville — at least in a position to shoot one final shot of the 4265 on the roll to East Deerfield. *(Jeffrey Plant)*

(Below) Road units in the maroon Minute Man scheme were infrequent on the West End in the 1960's, with the 1700's clearly ruling the roost. Around 1970 a number of the 1500-series GP-7's were sent to Mechanicville, working many of the local assignments handled by the aging NW-2's. In April 1971 good-looking GP-7's 1558-1575 are about four miles west of Mechanicville grinding upgrade at low speed with a long consist for Scotia and Rotterdam Junction. Notice how the B&M is using white paint when repainting the sides numbers on the maroon units. *(Jeffrey Plant)*

Minute Man Scheme

(Above) The intricate Minute Man and McGinnis paint schemes were expensive to maintain, so the B&M began to repaint units in the 1960's into a simple "Blue Dip" scheme. Noted rail photographer Jim Shaughnessy recorded F-7 #4268, the last B&M F-unit purchase, in the new scheme at Mechanicville engine terminal on February 15, 1969. (Jim Shaughnessy)

(Below) Jim was also on hand as repainted RS-3 #1506 headed the Rotterdam Junction local west on the joint B&M/D&H tracks west of Mechanicville at Coons, NY in the winter of 1969. RS-3's were rare on West End assignments such as this. (Jim Shaughnessy)

(Above) A snowy December day in 1969 finds units sporting a variety of paint schemes in the Mechanicville engine terminal. The simple all-blue schemes will win out, promising savings for a road that needs every spare dime to survive. *(Jeremy Plant)*

(Below) The New York Central operated a daily roundtrip freight between DeWitt Yard in Syracuse, NY and the B&M connection at Rotterdam Junction. Since Rotterdam lacked engine facilities, or most everything else, it was customary for the NYC engines to run through to Mechanicville and wait for the return trip at the engine terminal there. In August, 1967 an A-B-A set of Alco cab units is in the company of a set of Bluebird GP-9's. It's the last year of NYC's partnership with the B&M: Penn Central bows in later in the year. It will continue the operation to Mechanicville for the first years of P-C and then extend the run-through arrangement to points further east. The elderly cab units are common power on these trains, as are F's and RS-3's. *(Jeremy Plant)*

F-7 #4266A joined the B&M roster in 1949, working alongside Fox-trucked 2-6-0s and 2-8-0s dating back to the end of the prior century. Part of an order for four A-B sets — the only F-7s on the B&M — this sturdy and dependable EMD cab unit bucked the odds and remains active on the Conway Scenic Railroad. Usually assigned to the Conn River Line in the 1960's and early 1970's, in the winter of 1972-73 the F-7's began to appear frequently on the West End, sometimes as trailers on the pool freights with Penn Central. Wearing the plainest of blue dip paint and missing the reflectorized number board on its front door, #4266A is on the point of an East Deerfield to Mechanicville extra westbound, leading two GP-7s up the hill out of Greenfield on the afternoon of February 24, 1973. *(Jack Armstrong)*

Last of the F Units

(Above) In what must have been one of the last pure F-7 lashups on the B&M, #4266A-4265B-4265A are westbound at Charlemont on December 12, 1972 with another East Deerfield-Mechanicville extra. The old warriors are filling the Deerfield River Valley with the sweet music of 567 prime movers running flat out on the climb to Hoosac Tunnel. *(Jack Armstrong)*

(Below) On a lovely May morning in 1973, the 4266A and GP-9 1722 are leading two PC second generation units, #6087 and #6538, approaching Mechanicville with a westbound BM-7. *(Jeffrey Plant)*

(Above) On October 6, 1973, an eight-car train of RDC's headed by the 6153 is at the station site in North Adams to complete the second shuttle run of the day to Hoosac Tunnel. The Hoosac Mountains loom in the background, a barrier penetrable only by the 4.75 mile tunnel, longest in the nation from the time of its completion until 1916. The rows of unused catenary poles are reminders of the electrification zone that ended at the west here at North Adams, also site of the shops that serviced the electric engines. *(Charles Ballard)*

(Below) Three days later, an eastbound freight pulls by the old station location with a quartet of units repainted into the all-blue scheme: GP-9 #1724, F-7B #4266B, and GP-7's #1571 and 1572. The fall colors are ablaze on the Berkshires to the west, which presented no obstacle to the train's water-level passage up the valley of the Hoosic to the river's headwaters on Hoosac Mountain. *(Jack Armstrong)*

Rumors of new power for the B&M began building in 1972 and 1973, as the new management of the road began to develop strategies to stem the decline of the previous decade. A key ingredient was new motive power. The B&M was assigning its 1957 GP-9s and the six GP-18s of the 1961 order to its top trains, power that on other Class I roads was already relegated to secondary service. EMD's successful GP38-2 was a logical choice to succeed the first generation Geep's: cheap to buy, easy to maintain, dependable and rugged. The GP-38 was a real New England engine, too, already proven in years of service on the Maine Central and Bangor & Aroostook, two of the early purchasers of the type.

(Above) Upon delivery the 200's were assigned the glamour runs on the Fitchburg Division, such as TC-100 near North Adams behind the 210, named *Franklin Pierce* after New Hampshire's only president. The naming has a bit of irony attached, as many attributed Pierce's drinking problem and moodiness to grief over his son's death in a railroad accident. *(Jack Armstrong)*

(Below) The bridge over the Deerfield River at the east portal of Hoosac Tunnel has been a favorite location of photographers since the days of electrification. Few pictures have captured the feel of winter railroading in the mountains of New England as well as Bill Mischler's portrait of GP38-2's #201, 205, and 206 westbound on January 6, 1974. *(Bill Mischler)*

The 200's

(Above) SW-1 #1127 heads the once-a-week local on the Wheelwright Branch at Bondsville, MA on August 12, 1976. Time is running out for this western remnant of the Central Mass Branch, isolated from the eastern part by the floods of 1938. *(Charles Ballard)*

(Below) The 1500 received the dip paint job around 1970. In 1971 she is on one of her accustomed runs, the Peterboro Branch at Winchendon. By this time the Cheshire Branch that also served Winchendon is out of service. *(Bob Wilt Collection)*

(Above) The 1960's and 1970's were not kind to the B&M lines in New Hampshire. One after the other, they were sold, downgraded, left unused: the Cheshire, the Concord & Montreal, the Conway Branch, even the New Hampshire Mainline between Concord and White River Junction. This was a signalled, CTC-equipped mainline with over ten trains a day until the 1960's. In 1966 the decision was made to route traffic north by way of East Deerfield and the Connecticut River Line. The CTC was taken down and the New Hampshire Mainline became a marginal branch line, having little traffic production potential. By 1974, when Tom Post found the 1747 on the once-a-week Concord to White River Junction local at Lebanon, it was hard to realize that this was the path of the Boston AMBASSADORS and numerous milk and freight trains in days past. *(Tom Post)*

(Below) The success of the Vermont Railway in resuscitating traffic on the north-south route of the Rutland ensured a healthy interchange business with the B&M at North Bennington, VT. The station that had once hosted the MOUNT ROYAL and the GREEN MOUNTAIN FLYER on the Troy-Montreal run has been transformed by the village into a municipal office building, but the clock on the tower still tells the time as two B&M GP-9's are switching the Vermont interchange before returning to Mechanicville, January 22, 1978. *(Bill Mischler)*

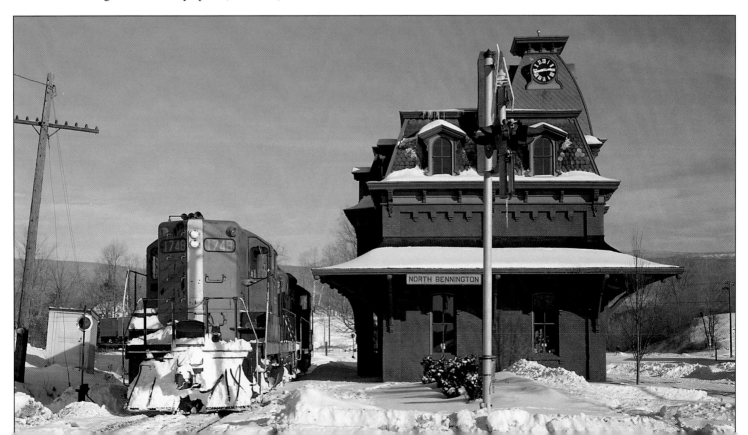

Connecticut Valley

(Above) It's September 30, 1972, and passenger service returns to the Connecticut River Line for the first time in six years. Amtrak's Washington to Montreal MONTREALER waits on CV tracks at the White River Junction station, having come up the Conn River Line from Springfield. The cupola of the 1938-built station is visible in the hazy summer night behind E-8 #4036 heading a three-unit lashup on the overnight run.

(Tom Post)

(Left) The arrival of the GP38-2's bumped enough GP-9's and GP-18's from Mechanicville runs to displace the first-generation power that had ruled the Conn River Line. The depot at Wells River, VT had over the years seen all manner of CP and B&M trains, and trains on the shortline Montpelier & Barre. In the summer of 1974 it was consumed by flames, leaving little but the charred wreckage GP-9 #1736 is passing on a southbound in July of that year. *(Tom Post)*

(Above) Continuing south at Newbury, VT the train passes through the beautiful section of the Connecticut Valley that Dr. Phil Hastings, a native of the region, had immortalized in his splendid black-and-white photography two decades earlier.

(Tom Post)

(Below) Besides the through route to Canada via the CP the Conn River Line afforded access to the paper industry of Northern New Hampshire. A daily freight between White River Junction and Berlin, NH followed the Conn River to Wells River, seen here at North Thetford, VT behind GP-18 #1752. *(Tom Post)*

East Deerfield

(Above) East Deerfield, at the intersection of the B&M's two busiest lines, was the most popular location on the railroad for railfans to congregate. The legendary "Railfan Bridge" on the west side of the yard afforded good overhead shots of trains entering and leaving the yard, as seen here on August 2, 1974. GP-18 #1754 heads an eastbound into the yard alongside a switch cut with an Alco switcher (a type commonly found working at East Deerfield in the 1970's). To the left two tracks branch off: in the foreground is the "Loop" leading to the Connecticut River Line, and farther back is the switchback to the Turners Falls Branch. (Jack Armstrong)

(Above) Looking east from the bridge we see approaching an Ayer-Mechanicville extra with B&M #1727 leading Conrail #3687 on February 17, 1979.

(Jack Armstrong)

(Above) Connecticut River Line train JS-2 is coming down the Loop behind maroon GP-7 #1560 and GP-9 #1744 in March of 1978. The Conn River Line was the traditional bumping ground for the older power on the system right up to Guilford days. *(Gardiner Cross)*

(Below) The Turners Falls Branch was a former New Haven line that the B&M used to reach its namesake town, just north of Greenfield on the east bank of the Connecticut. Alco switchers were the usual power on the Turner Falls local freight E-6, seen here on a sunny April 23, 1976 cutting through the greens of the local golf course. *(Matthew Herson)*

(Above) Jeremy Plant was returning to Schenectady on an August evening in 1976 after a productive afternoon chasing the Green Mountain Railroad in Vermont. Finding a green signal on the westbound track at Eagle Bridge he decided to wait a few minutes at East Buskirk for the shot. What should appear but ex-EL F-7 #7131 on the point of BM-7. A late-summer thunderstorm has cleared the air as the train arrives at Mechanicville.
(Jeremy Plant)

(Below) The dominance of the 1700's on through B&M freights in the 1970's cut down on the number of surprises a railfan could expect on the east-west mainlines, with the major exception of runthrough power. In addition to the Bow coal trains the most likely candidates for non-B&M power were the western connection trains to and from Dewitt Yard in Syracuse. Until the early 1970's these trains had used NYC and PC power only as far as Mechanicville, where they were serviced and turned for the trip back on home rails. Changes in operating philosophy led to the demand for longer runs to utilize power more efficiently, and so PC and later Conrail power became daily visitors to B&M rails. Cab units were the favored power in the last days of the NYC and well into the Penn Central era. An example is shown here as westbound BM-7, led by ex-NYC F-7s 1832-1829-1839, heads out of East Deerfield under the railfan bridge on June 24, 1974. *(Jack Armstrong)*

(Above) The eastbound daytime counterpart of BM-7 was NY-10. NY-10 usually arrived at Rotterdam Junction late in the morning and around mid-day entered the flow of traffic on the B&M/D&H joint line. At Crescent, a few miles east of Schenectady, an NY-10 behind ex-NYC U25B #2507, an ex-EL U25B and a leased SP&S RS-3 has gotten the green signal after waiting for the southbound ADIRONDACK with PA-4s to run past it on the D&H track in the background that merges here with the B&M for the run to "Mickeyville." It's just the last week in September but the trees in this swampy location are already starting to blaze red and orange. *(Jeremy Plant)*

(Below) B&M units were also common on the pooled-power trains and ran west of Rotterdam Junction to Dewitt and points west. On a morning in November, 1976 NY-10 is entering the city of Amsterdam, the last town before Rotterdam Junction, from the west on the ex-NYC mainline behind freshly painted GP-9 #1704 and ex-EL and PC GE's. *(Jeremy Plant)*

New Englanders date the American Revolution to 1775, the year of "the shots heard round the world" and the Battle of Bunker Hill. So it was no great surprise that the B&M beat the official 1976 Bicentennial celebration by a year by repainting GP38-2 #212 into a handsome red-white-blue scheme and renumbering it #200. (The number sequence for the 12 GP38-2s had begun with #201.) Orders were given to put the flashy "Flag" on the point whenever possible — and more often than not, in these years of high morale and good feeling on the B&M, it was found there.

(Above) A week before the 200th anniversary of Lexington and Concord the 200 is leading the American Freedom Train and ex-Reading T-1 4-8-4 #2101 over the Hoosic River between Williamstown and North Adams toward the festivities in eastern Massachusetts. *(Gardiner Cross)*

(Right) At the most famous location on the system the 200 heads out of the East Portal of Hoosac Tunnel in May of 1976.

(Jim Odell)

(Right) By all standards the 200 was one of the few esthetic triumphs of American railroading's effort to get into the Bicentennial spirit by repainting engines in patriotic garb. The B&M managed to express the red-white-blue flag motif in a way that complemented the angular and simple lines of a non-dynamic brake equipped GP38-2. The stars-and-stripes front-end treatment fit beautifully with the simple bold color panels on the sides. The 200 looked especially striking outlined against the dark trees lining the right of way near the Westvaco plant in Mechanicville, eastbound on the approach to the Hudson River bridge.

(Jeremy Plant)

(Above) An eastbound Bow coal train is roughly at the point where New York and Vermont meet in April 1977. Before single-tracking the two tracks of the mainline here, between Petersburgh Junction and North Pownal, were on opposite sides of the Hoosic. This train's power captures much of the history of B&M paint schemes for road freight power: bicentennial, solid blue, McGinnis, Minute Man. *(Jeffrey Plant)*

(Below) In early April of 1976 the 200 leads NE-84 east into Schaghticoke, where it will meet and follow the Hoosic River to its headwaters near Hoosac Tunnel. It's the month of change for most railroads in the Northeast, as Conrail emerges from the ashes of bankrupt carriers and neighbor D&H adds new engines and route miles, but B&M soldiers on without dramatic immediate changes under the able leadership of Alan Dustin. *(Jeremy Plant)*

In the days of steam on the West End B&M 2-10-2's were the usual power on the trains to the New York Central's Selkirk Yard outside Albany. The B&M trains would go west to Rotterdam Junction, out onto the West Shore Freight Line to a connection at Hoffmans with the passenger line through Schenectady. Passing Schenectady they would then head south on the Carman Cutoff to the freight line for the trip into Selkirk. By the 1970's the passenger line no longer saw freights, and B&M trains to Selkirk would move out onto the CTC-controlled Conrail mainline, detach and change tracks on the crossovers at Hoffmans, hook up again and head toward Selkirk. It took a bit of time, a caboose on each end of the train, and of course it fouled both tracks of a busy mainline. Crews got to know the Mohawk River well, crossing it three times (once on B&M, twice on Conrail) each trip.

(Above) On a May day in 1976 the 1706 is running long-end forward leading four other 1700's past the small Conrail yard and "Mt. Saltmore." In the background is the ridge of the Helderberg Mountains, part of the Catskill range. Out of sight at a lower level is the mainline of the Delaware & Hudson between Schenectady and Binghamton, roughly at the point where the end of the train is curving into view. The run-around procedure is undoubtedly the reason for the unusual sight of a B&M Geep running long-end forward on a road freight assignment. *(Jeremy Plant)*

Selkirk Connection

Selkirk Yard occupied (and still does) one of the most strategic locations on Conrail and its predecessor roads, Penn Central and New York Central. Central's ownership of both the former West Shore lines and the original New York & Hudson River line up the east bank of the Hudson allowed it to utilize the West Shore lines for freight traffic, keep it out of the way of most passengers, and avoid the stiff grade the passenger trains confronted leaving Albany and the Hudson Valley for the west. Just east of the yard is the junction of the Boston and Albany mainline and the West Shore (the so-called "River Line") to New Jersey. A line from the Port of Albany (once used by NYC passenger trains on the West Shore) also joins here. B&A trains and freights on the Water Level Route to Manhattan cross the Hudson on the Alfred Smith Bridge, with the connection to the Water Level Route branching off at the east end of the bridge and joining the mainline at Stuyvesant. B&M access to Selkirk complemented its connection with the D&H at Mechanicville in providing north-south connections for its traffic. B&M GP-9 #1722 leads another four-unit consist into the yard in May, 1976. *(Jeffrey Plant)*

(Above) A number of units received partial Bicentennial schemes in the bicentennial years 1975-77. A simple red/white/blue set of nose stripes and a black Minute Man silhouette did wonders for the simple blue and white Geeps. GP-9 #1737 is at the Mechanicville engine terminal in November 1977 wearing the nose stripes and Minute Man. (Gardiner Cross)

(Below) The low-nosed GP-18's were easy to modify with the striped front end. The 1751 waits for a crew to head east from the small yard at Rotterdam Junction. (Jeremy Plant)

Bicentennial Geeps

Built in 1850 as the Ashuelot Railroad and acquired by the B&M in 1893 as part of the purchase of the Connecticut River Railroad, the 22-mile Ashuelot Branch followed its namesake river from Dole Junction, NH northeast to Keene, the major city of southwestern New Hampshire, where it connected with the Cheshire Branch. Abandonment of the old B&M mainline up the east side of the Connecticut River from East Northfield to Dole Junction in favor of the CV line on the west side made the Ashuelot trains the only traffic on the remaining section of the line from Brattleboro down to Dole Jct. and connection with the branch, renamed the Fort Hill Branch. Abandonment of the Cheshire in 1972 (after several years of little or no service) left the Ashuelot as Keene's only rail connection. Light rail on the branch dictated use of light power, usually a single SW-9.

(Above and below) A book on the B&M without a picture of a covered bridge would be unthinkable. Jim Shaughnessy was on hand to capture the 1225 and its train at the covered bridge at Ashuelot, NH spanning the river of the same name. It's March of the snowy winter of 1977, and the snowcover is beginning to melt in the late-winter sun. It will soon be time for tapping the maples in Northern New England. *(Both, Jim Shaughnessy)*

Ashuelot Branch

(Above) Maroon SW-9 #1220 is on the point of local E-8 to Keene on June 19, 1979 at Winchester, NH, almost the midway point between Brattleboro and Keene. *(Jack Armstrong)*

(Below) On March 28, 1978, #1231 again has the Ashuelot assignment, seen here at Keene preparing to return to Brattleboro with four boxcars and a caboose. In just few years, traffic levels on the branch will see a precipitous drop, leading to the decision to lease the line to the Green Mountain Railroad to operate. *(Jack Armstrong)*

Until the arrival of 18 GP40-2's, #300-#317, in the last days of 1977 and early January 1978, the B&M rostered nothing more powerful than the 2,000 horsepower GP38-2's bought in 1973. The higher horsepower 300's were expected to speed up times on the major bridge routes essential to the prosperity of the road. All sorts of rumors circulated in late 1977 about possible paint schemes for the new units, with a real hope held out for a return to the Minute Man scheme or something non-blue in wake of the Conrail decision to paint their engines in a blue-and-white scheme similar to the B&M's. In the end, the new 3,000 horsepower units represented only an incremental improvement over the stark scheme of the 200's, inaugurating the large block lettering on the nose and the flanks of the engines. The 300's were handsome engines, but left open the question why the B&M didn't choose this time to create a new image clearly different from that of competitor Conrail.

(Above) January 2, 1978, finds Mechanicville engine terminal well-stocked with the road's new flagship power. Modelers not wanting to weather their Athearn GP40-2's can certainly duplicate this day's activities, although the 304 is already showing the usual traces of sand on its front truck and cab. *(Jeremy Plant)*

(Left) Shortly after delivery the 300 was named the *John W. Barriger* after the legendary railroad executive who served as B&M's president from 1971 to 1973. Barriger was considered a "railroader's railroader," an advocate of industry modernization who took on some of the toughest jobs around: making marginal railroads like the Monon, Rock Island, Katy, and B&M survive in the harsh world of mergers and intermodal competition.

(Jim Shaughnessy)

(Left) Late on the afternoon of January 2, 1978 the trio of 304-313-314 is hard at work lifting an eastbound freight from Mechanicville up the grade into Schaghticoke, NY. Credit Jim Odell for this superb backlit winter shot. The angle shows well how the B&M continued to eschew options on its second-generation EMD power: no sunshades on the cab windows and no dynamic brakes. But the crew is assuredly happy that management decided to fork over the money for pilot snowplows. *(James Odell)*

(Above) For the next few years the B&M tended to run the 300's in solid sets, thus making maximum use of their high-horsepower capabilities. The warmer air of March meeting the frozen earth and snow has filled the upper Hudson Valley with a late-winter fog that has frozen on the trees and clings ominously to the riverbank on this morning in 1978. At Hemstreet Park, across the river from Mechanicville, the combination of higher elevation and the sun breaking through the mist provides perfect lighting for an eastbound behind the set of 310-302-317. The placement of the side numbers on these units makes them easy to identify from the 3/4 angle.
(Jeffrey Plant)

BOSTON & MAINE...
TIES TO
NEW ENGLAND
AND CANADA

(Below) In a classic scene of New England winter railroading, Bob Wilt found the 316 on the lead of BM-7 westbound at Ayer on March 1, 1978. (Bob Wilt)

(Above) In a very different role the 311 and 313 are at Waltham bringing the Ringling Brothers - Barnum & Bailey circus train the last few miles into Boston on October 23, 1979. This circus made an annual late autumn appearance at Boston Garden and the train became a yearly feature of trainwatching in the Boston area. *(Bob Wilt collection)*

(Below) The bright blue-and-white scheme of the 300's looked almost as sharp against the bareness of a snowless winter day as it did in the white stuff. Witness the trio of 304-316-310 lifting a westbound Conrail connection out of the yard at Mechanicville and toward Rotterdam Jct. on a December, 1978 afternoon. The B&M in the Dustin years found a winning formula with the three-unit sets of 300's, a perfect combination of speed and power for the B&M's needs. *(Jack Armstrong)*

(Opposite page) At the West Portal of Hoosac, the 309 emerges with a westbound behind the typical three-unit set of 300's on June 22, 1980. *(Jack Armstrong)*

Until the 1970's CP Rail power on Conn River Line trains rarely ventured south of White River Junction. As the railroad industry in general embraced the concept of longer runs and fewer crew and engine changes the anachronistic division of the Montreal-Springfield run into CV, CP, and B&M sections was more and more uneconomical. Runthrough power on Springfield-White River Junction-Newport trains and CV-B&M pooling on the St. Albans-Springfield route became more prevalent.

(Above) On August 8, 1971, a southbound CP freight from Newport has arrived at White River Junction behind an RS-18/RS-10/RS-3 lashup. The Alco's will turn their train over to the waiting B&M crew in the GP-7's for the run south to Springfield. *(George Berisso)*

(Right) The B&M also pooled power with Central Vermont between Springfield and St. Albans, VT. Grand Trunk GP-9 #4445 leads two B&M Geeps on a northbound at Deerfield, MA in March, 1978.

(Gardiner Cross)

(Above) Another SJ-1 is at Greenfield heading north behind two CP RS-18s bracketing the 1721. On CP, eastern Canada and New England was Alco/MLW territory almost exclusively, so much of the power assigned to the power pool was Alco, much to the delight of railfans. The mainline to Mechanicville is in the foreground, curving away to the west. *(James Odell)*

(Below) Northbound train SJ-1 crosses the Connecticut River at Holyoke behind CP C424 #4202 and two B&M Geeps on April 1, 1978. The power will continue on to Newport. *(James Odell)*

Compared to other railroads operating money-losing commuter passenger service the B&M fared well. The Commonwealth of Massachusetts, perhaps realizing how incapable it was of providing the roads to handle the rush of commuters descending daily on downtown Boston, had since 1964 subsidized area commuter service. The MBTA, the state's vehicle for this, was also in the process of purchasing the B&M's commuter lines in the early 1970's, part of the package needed to get the road out of bankruptcy. Conrail's desire to not be involved in commuter operations (and what the MBTA considered to be excessive charges to handle its ex-NYC and NH commuter operations) led to an expanded role for the B&M in 1977, handling under contract both the South Station and North Station commuter operations.

BOSTON and MAINE CORPORATION

PASSENGER TRAIN SCHEDULES
BOSTON AND MAINE CORPORATION
Robert N. Reserve and Benjamin H. Lacy, Trustees

TIMETABLE NO.
20

REVISED JULY 1, 1974
EASTERN STANDARD TIME
APRIL 29, 1973

GEORGE F. GALLAGHER
Superintendent
North Station, Boston, 02114

INFORMATION 227-5070

(Above) The MBTA's lease of the D&H's four PA's at the end of the summer of 1977 produced one of the alltime great trains on the B&M. Eastbound AP-4 out of Mechanicville has all four of the Alco cabs leading three B&M Geeps at Schaghticoke, NY. The PA's were no strangers to freight service, having finished their days on the D&H hauling freights on the Champlain Division after being bumped from passenger service in February 1977 by Turboliners. The PA's were not assigned to the ex-B&M lines out of North Station, but worked out of South Station before being shipped to Mexico in 1978.

(Jim Shaughnessy)

B&M equipment started to show up at South Station after the agreement with MBTA. RDC-3 #6302 is on the rear of train #800 from Stoughton, posing near the distinctive lower quadrant semaphores at Bridge 9, South Station, on June 11, 1979. *(J. W. Swanberg)*

(Below) At South Station, B&M SW-1 #1122 shares duties with the garish ex-GM&O FP-10's purchased by the MBTA through trade-ins of 19 ex-New Haven GP-9's. Called "Easter Eggs" because of their colors on the bulldog nose, the F's and 18 F-40PH's purchased new by the Authority formed the mainstay of the commuter fleet in Boston, the fourth-largest commuter rail operation in the country in daily passenger count. *(J. W. Swanberg)*

(Right) A short-lived experiment was Fiat railcar #668-920, used on North Station runs in the mid-1970's for a year. The unit was a throwback to the doodlebug gas-electrics of the prewar days, but with a certain European air. The little train is seen at Chelsea, MA in August of 1976.

(Russell Munroe)

(Above) The B&M was adding as well as subtracting its branch lines in the Hoosic Valley. It acquired the 18 mile former NYC branch from Pittsfield to North Adams along with several former Conrail (New Haven) branches in Connecticut in the early 1980's. Local freight ME-2 with GP-9's #1723-1717 is southbound at Hodges Crossing near North Adams on October 10, 1983. The B&M operated the branch from its northern terminus at North Adams and rarely ventured all the way to Pittsfield at the southern end.

(Jack Armstrong)

(Above) As Guilford Transportation came closer to finalizing the takeover of the MEC-B&M-D&H group of railroads, marginal lines were sold. In the Hoosic region, the Battenkill Railroad was formed to operate two interconnected D&H properties, the Washington Branch from its connection with the B&M mainline at Eagle Bridge, NY to Salem Junction, and the D&H-owned shortline Greenwich & Johnsonville that ran from the Hudson River at Thompson to a connection with the D&H at Salem Junction. The elimination of the Washington Branch north of Salem meant that the B&M connection at Eagle Bridge was the new road's only link to the outside. On the first day of Battenkill operation, August 16, 1982, a train led by B&M GP-9 #1732 and Battenkill RS-3 #4119 (ex-G&J, originally D&H) is leaving B&M tracks and heading onto the new shortline, still in operation as this book is written. (Jeffrey Plant)

(Opposite page) Another change in the Hoosic Valley in 1982 was the acquisition of the 6.8 mile branch from the New York/Vermont border at White Creek/North Bennington to the B&M mainline at Hoosick Junction, in the town of Hoosick west of Hoosick Falls. Interchange with the B&M would thereafter take place at Hoosick Junction, freeing the B&M from the need to maintain the deteriorating track of the branch and run locals to meet the Vermont train from Rutland. The Vermont's RS-3 #603 is crossing the Walloomsac River bridge at North Hoosick in September of 1982, one of two bridges on the branch over this stream. It is proceeding slowly and cautiously over the rapids, with track speed down to 10 miles per hour on the undermaintained rails.

(Jeffrey Plant)

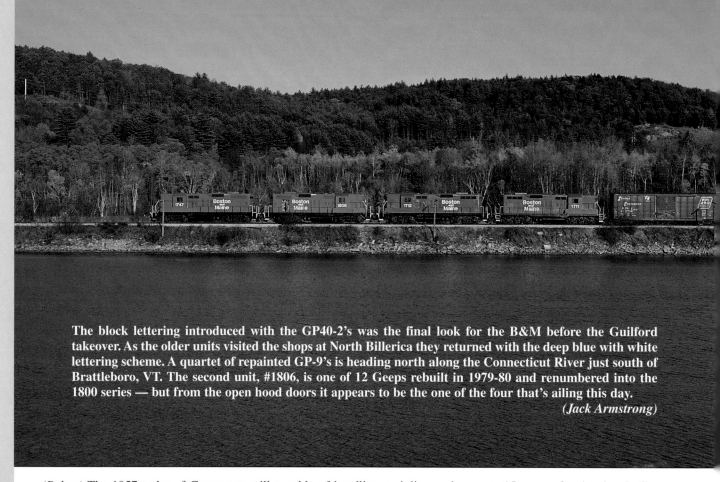

The block lettering introduced with the GP40-2's was the final look for the B&M before the Guilford takeover. As the older units visited the shops at North Billerica they returned with the deep blue with white lettering scheme. A quartet of repainted GP-9's is heading north along the Connecticut River just south of Brattleboro, VT. The second unit, #1806, is one of 12 Geeps rebuilt in 1979-80 and renumbered into the 1800 series — but from the open hood doors it appears to be the one of the four that's ailing this day.

(Jack Armstrong)

(Below) The 1957 order of Geeps was still capable of handling mainline assignments 15 years after leaving LaGrange. Three of the GP-9's team up with a GP-7, all in the new scheme, to lift the Mount Tom coal train up the grade out of the Hudson Valley at Hemstreet Park in September, 1982. *(James Odell)*

(Above) The GP-18's also got the new scheme. By the 1980's the original low-nosed units on the road had been relegated to locals and other lesser assignments along with the GP-9's. The 1752 is heading west from Mechanicville at the first Coons Crossing with the local to Rotterdam Junction. *(Jack Wright)*

(Below) In a different corner of the system the 1754 is at the ball signal guarding the crossing of the Maine Central and B&M at Whitefield, NH. It's September 1982, and the Whitefield balls are the last of their kind still in operation. The two-ball signal indicates clear for the Maine Central tracks, on which the GP-18 is switching cars. *(Jim Shaughnessy)*

Timothy Mellon's acquisition of the Maine Central in June, 1981 put Guilford Transportation into the New England railroad business and presaged the subsequent acquisition of Delaware and Hudson and B&M. In August 1982, even before the consummation of the impending B&M purchase, MEC units began run-through operations over the rails of their future merger partners. The handsome and well-maintained Harvest Yellow Downeasters added a new element to railfanning on the B&M, contrasting vividly with the blue units of the host road.

(Above) Maine Central was one of the first buyers of EMD's highly successful GP-38 model, replacing its cab units with a dozen of the 2,000 horsepower units in 1966. A pure four-unit set is leading Mechanicville-Portland train MEPO east through Hoosick Falls, NY in the first month of the power pool arrangement, at a time when pure sets of MEC power were the order of the day. *(James Odell)*

(Below) Another MEPO is in the clear at North Adams with a mixture of B&M and MEC units on a September day in 1982. Train POSE heads west for the Conrail connection with a three unit set of MEC GP-38's. Three decades have passed since MEC power, then in the form of passenger E-7s in the Boston-Troy power pool, appeared on these rails. *(James Odell)*

The Maine Central Arrives

(Above) Maine Central U25B #232 is at the westernmost point of the B&M as it approaches the Conrail mainline at Rotterdam Junction with POSE on a sunny December afternoon in 1983. The U25B is one of a group purchased from the leaseholders of the Rock Island's large stable of this type in 1981. Although B&M never ordered this pioneer GE model, it was no stranger to B&M rails as a common type of unit for the NYC-PC-Conrail power pools over the years. *(Jeffrey Plant)*

(Below) On the last day of 1983, P&LE U28B's are sandwiched by two B&M units on a westbound at Eagle Bridge, NY. The P&LE units were becoming common on the B&M by the time of the Guilford acquisition, often straying from the coal trains and showing up on other consists. *(James Odell)*

(Above) Her glory days as the gaudy Flag unit over, GP38-2 #200 is wearing the original plain-Jane blue scheme she was delivered in as #212. The only odd touch is the blue numberboards from the bicentennial scheme. By this time, the winter of 1983, most B&M units had received the block letter scheme. The 200 is leading two Conrail units west at Valley Falls, NY over the cold waters of the Hoosic River.
(Jeffrey Plant)

(Below) October 12, Columbus Day, is the traditional day for leaf-watching in New England: the colors are usually at their peak. Columbus Day 1982 in Western Massachusetts is still far from peak. Train SPPO has come up from Springfield on the Conn River Line and is proceeding east through Montague on the Fitchburg on its run to Rigby Yard. A few early-turning maples make a vivid contrast to the almost identical blue and white colors of B&M #202 and Conrail #1994.
(Jack Armstrong)

(Above) Along with several other railroads the B&M experimented with the use of a road slug to add tractive effort to power consists. The slug, #100 and class MT-4, was built at North Billerica in February 1983 from Union Pacific GP-9 #134. The slug provided tractive effort from its powered traction motors and was mated to GP40-2's #300-301. The set was used on road freights, as here at XO Tower, Mechanicville, about to enter the D&H yard with a westbound.

(James Odell)

(Below) In the summer of 1983 pushers were occasionally used on the West End, pushing out of Mechanicville east to East Deerfield. GP-9 #1741 is pushing hard on Mechanicville-Lawrence train MELA at North Adams in August 1983, its new paint already weathered like a pair of well-worn jeans. *(James Odell)*

Space permits only a sampling of Guilford operations on former B&M lines. With the acquisition of Delaware & Hudson in January of 1984 the Guilford system, MEC-B&M-D&H, was complete, and the system began to look and operate more like a single railroad. Despite drastic declines in traffic on all the former B&M routes, trainwatching in the Guilford era had its appeal: new color schemes, new types of engines, all sorts of combinations, new train operations.

(Above) Pittsburgh & Lake Erie #2818 leads five mates splicing a single Guilford EMD eastbound at Hemstreet Park in January, 1985. *(Jeffrey Plant)*

(Above) Six-axle power began appearing in the late 1980's as Guilford went the second-hand locomotive market route. Colorful additions were the SD-26's acquired from Santa Fe. Rebuilt from SD-24's, they introduced a new engine type to New England. Before repainting, yellow-bonnets #4675-4641 head east at the "Brickyard" on the east side of the Hudson River Bridge. *(Jeffrey Plant)*

(Below) The 632 heads two U33C's, one ex-Conrail and one ex-D&H, at the East Portal in April 1987.
(Jeffrey Plant)

Guilford

(Above) The evening light catches a trio of ex-B&M 300's on BADH crossing the Merrimack River at Haverhill, MA. The orange stripe of the Guilford scheme really showed up well in low-light pictures such as this. The all-B&M matched consist was unusual on a road that mixed and matched all sorts of oddball power by this time. A generous arrangement with MBTA allowed this stretch of the freight mainline to host both freight and passenger trains. This train is down from Rigby and will follow the old Western Route mainline as far as Lowell Junction, where it will swing to the west to head out to East Deerfield. (Gardiner Cross)

(Below) The largest Guilford engines were the SD-45's acquired from Norfolk Southern. Along with ex-N&W GP-35's they brought high short hoods back to a road that had been among the first in the East to acquire low-nosed GP-18's. The 687 leads a seven-unit consist eastbound through Mechanicville with a Bow coal train bound for New Hampshire's Merrimack Valley. By the time of this shot in November 1989, the diamonds at XO were gone, and the former D&H and B&M yards at Mechanicville were largely empty. (Brian Plant)

(*Above*) Eastern commuter operations provided the last great stand of F-units in North America. Well into the 1980's and 1990's the bulldog noses of F's could still be seen hauling commuters out of Boston, New York, New Jersey, Baltimore, and Washington. The Western Route of the B&M through Reading provided one of the best locations to shoot cab units. In 1988, 42 trains a day powered by F's operated on the line, due to a clearance restriction that prevented the MBTA's F-40PH's from the line. FP-10 #1104, one of 19 former GM&O F-3's rebuilt into 1,800 horse-power units at ICG's Paducah, KY, Shops, leads a train of Pullman-Standard cars at Cedar Park Station, Melrose, on May 15, 1988. (*Gardiner Cross*)

(*Below*) In a setting made famous in earlier days by shots of the MOUNTAINEER and Moguls on commuter trains, #1151 leads a train of depowered Budds south along Crystal Lake in Wakefield on a sparkling late-autumn day in 1988. (*Gardiner Cross*)

MBTA

(Above) The FP-10's shared MBTA duties with 18 F-40PH's purchased new in 1978 and 1980. In the summer of 1989 a southbound behind F-40 #1067 is crossing venerable draw-bridge #7 at Everett on the Eastern. The bridge dated back to the 1890's, and in a few weeks is slated for replacement by the new bridge visible to the left of the picture. *(Gardiner Cross)*

(Below) Another train of Budds is seen on a Lowell run at Montvale Avenue in Woburn in November 1988. *(Gardiner Cross)*

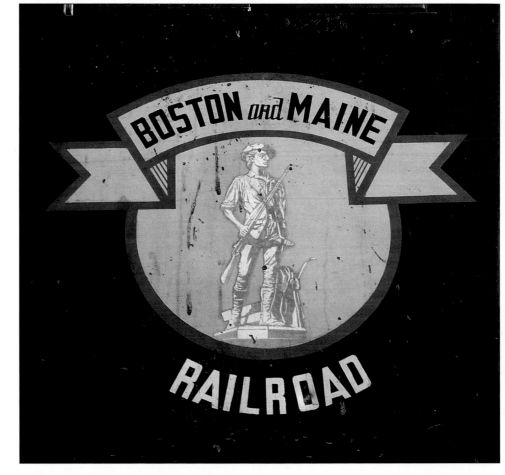

Farewell

(Above) The B&M of memo-
ries: P-3-a Pacific #3701 at
Boston in 1951, resplendent in
striped lettering, an elegant
reminder of the glory years of
the Boston & Maine.
(James Buckley)

(Right) The Minute Man:
symbol of the Boston &
Maine. The figure was sculpt-
ed by Daniel Chester French
in 1875 for Concord, MA's
centennial celebration of the
Revolution. It was French's
first major commission. This
and his magnificent seated
Lincoln in the Lincoln
Memorial in Washington are
his most famous works.
(William J. Brennan)